Elements of Article Writing Series

QUERIES & SUBMISSIONS

THOMAS CLARK

WRITER'S DIGEST BOOKS
CINCINNATI, OHIO

Queries & Submissions. Copyright © 1995 by Thomas Clark. Printed and bound in the United States of America. All rights reserved. No part of this book may be reproduced in any form or by any electronic or mechanical means including information storage and retrieval systems without permission in writing from the publisher, except by a reviewer, who may quote brief passages in a review. Published by Writer's Digest Books, an imprint of F&W Publications, Inc., 1507 Dana Avenue, Cincinnati, Ohio 45207. (800) 289-0963. First edition.

This hardcover edition of *Queries & Submissions* features a "self-jacket" that eliminates the need for a separate dust jacket. It provides sturdy protection for your book while it saves paper, trees and energy.

Other fine Writer's Digest Books are available from your local bookstore or direct from the publisher.

99 98 97 96 95   5 4 3 2 1

Library of Congress Cataloging-in-Publication Data

Clark, Thomas
    Queries & submissions / Thomas Clark.
        p.   cm.—(Elements of article writing series)
    Includes index.
    ISBN 0-89879-660-1 (alk. paper)
    1. Queries (Authorship) 2. Authorship—Marketing. 3. Feature writing. I. Title.
    II. Series.
PN161.C55 1995
808'.02—dc20   95-16594
                                                                    CIP

Edited by Roseann Biederman
Designed by Brian Roeth and Sandy Conopeotis Kent
Cover illustration by Sandy Conopeotis Kent

For Peggy,
as is everything;

and for Brittany, Brad and Jeff,
who teach me so much

ACKNOWLEDGMENTS

Nearly a dozen years ago, I remember asking my wife how you go about writing a letter to apply for a job you know you're not qualified for. I don't remember her exact words, but they were something along the lines of, "Well, you don't say that!" Whatever I wrote was good enough: I got the assignment. And I've been an editor at *Writer's Digest* ever since.

I've been blessed in more ways than I can count through that association. But most of all I benefited from working for a man who wasn't just a boss, but also a good friend. Bill Brohaugh finally "beat the newspaper out of me," and along the way he shared a lot of baseball, beer, Szechwan chicken and editorial savvy. He even figured out a way to get a book out of me. It meant him leaving *Writer's Digest* to become editorial director of Writer's Digest Books, of course, but . . . well, whatever works.

All I can say is "Thanks."

I am also indebted to the other men and women with whom I've worked at *Writer's Digest*: Rose Adkins, Sharon Rudd, Bill Strickland, Bruce Woods, Angela Terez, Jo Gilbert, Amanda Boyd, and a league of editorial assistants and interns. And even Pete Blocksom, who never though he'd get his name on an Acknowledgments page. In the process of putting out the world's leading magazine for writers, each shared insights and opinions and tips that are wrapped up in the advice I've put my name to in these pages.

The same goes to the authors whose articles have appeared in *Writer's Digest* during the past dozen years. On your way to helping *WD*'s readers, you gave me a matchless education, too.

You'll meet a few of them in this book, along with several other writers who graciously allowed me to share with you their successful letters to editors. Their help was invaluable in the writing of this book—as was my stack of Windham Hill CDs. Do you know what the sound of one man typing is? A sound in desperate search of a soundtrack, believe me.

Once the book got out of my basement office, it went into the caring hands of Jack Heffron and Roseann Biederman at Writer's Digest

Books. Editors humor themselves by assuming their writing doesn't need an editor—after all, one's been working on it from the beginning. If I harbored such delusions, Jack and Roseann helped me to appreciate anew just how valuable additional sets of eyes can be.

Finally, at the risk of sounding like an overwrought actor at the Academy Awards, I must acknowledge six more vital contributors to this book. My parents, Bill and Lorraine, raised me in a home where books and magazines lived also and where reading was an honorable use of time. Quite literally, that early habit led me to where I am today.

It would make a great story to say I met Peggy in a bookstore (actually, it was a speech festival), so we've settled for piling enough books and magazines into our home to have it mistaken for one. In the process, we've had the privilege of passing along a love and respect for words on paper to our children, Brittany, Brad and Jeff. Enough respect for them to understand why Dad spends a whole lot of evenings in the basement typing. I hope all four of them find this book worthy of their patience.

Thomas Clark
January 1995

Author's Note: In writing this book, I definitively concluded that "he or she" and "his or her" are the most awkward constructions ever devised, with the possible exception of "s/he." Therefore, I've used masculine pronouns when referring to a writer and feminine pronouns when referring to an editor. Unless, of course, the pronouns refer to real-life individuals, whom I've graciously allowed to retain their gender (myself included).

TABLE OF CONTENTS

CHAPTER ONE

This Really Is Important

The ability to write a winning query letter is the most important sales tool an article writer can acquire.

Whoa! Talk about your bold first sentences! But that's not first paragraph posturing or ill-considered hyperbole. A successful query letter gets the client to say "Yes." And that's the only real goal of any sales tool.

For you, the freelance writer, the "client" is an editor, specifically, the editor in charge of making article assignments at the magazine you want to write for. *You* are the salesperson, the one with a product to sell. That product is the article you will write from the idea you created. How you came to develop that idea and how you decided which editor should receive the idea are also important marketing considerations—no doubt about it. We'll look at both in this book, but they are secondary tools nonetheless. But most important is the letter in which you outline your specific article idea for the editor and state your credentials to write this piece. In industry parlance, it's a "query letter," and it alone will either clinch the sale (that is, win you the assignment) or bring home your SASE with a curt note concerning your inability to meet the editor's current needs.

I hear your challenge already: "But what about the article? Isn't writing the article more important than the query letter?"

In a longer view, of course it is. But I said the query letter is your most important *sales tool*. Remember, your article is product; delivering a publishable article falls under the category of service/customer satisfaction. (Creating such an article is the topic of several other books in this series.) But you'll never get the chance to serve your client if you don't sell her first.

And that's why you—the would-be successful freelance article writer—must learn to write effective, enticing, "yes"-producing query letters.

To *Freshwater & Marine Aquarium Magazine*

It's the first thing you see when you walk into the room. Your eyes are drawn like a magnet to the tank as they take in the fish, the plants and all that water. It's like no other tank you've ever seen in real life: It's luscious, it's beautiful, and it seems bigger than the entire couch and kitchen table put together! With a sigh of envy, you realize you're in the presence of the dream of most aquarium owners—that breed of tank bigger than fifty-five gallons. As you lose yourself watching the fish, you swear under your breath that someday you're going to have one of these.

Sound familiar? It will to most aquarium owners who can recall the first time they saw a monster tank in real life. I'd like to write a 500- to 1,000-word article on "Monster Tanks: Moving Up to the Pros." The piece would cover the following:

- why anyone would want a tank larger than fifty-five gallons;
- where someone would get a monster tank, what sizes are available today, and what it's going to cost him;
- what to look for when considering buying a huge aquarium;
- precautions to beware of when moving and setting up a 1,000-plus pound tank;
- factors to consider when planning your new equipment and maintenance needs; and
- a summary of tips for anyone thinking of taking the plunge (no pun intended) into the world of monster tanks.

As a resource for this piece, I've already arranged an interview with Jerry Ritzow, president of the Allglass Aquarium Company. I can have the article finished within two weeks and would like to be considered for an assignment.

I have successfully maintained several aquariums, both fresh and marine, for the past five years and am currently a master's student in biology at Indiana University of Pennsylvania. In addition to selling an article to *Tropical Fish Hobbyist*, I also sold a piece to you titled "How to Train Your Oscar" about three weeks ago.

I look forward to your response.

Sincerely,

Mark R. Feil

To *Friendly Exchange*

Oregon Territory! A hundred and fifty years ago it sounded like nirvana. Only trouble was, its fabled natural riches lay 2,100 miles from the nearest civilized outpost. Yet from 1843 to 1869, almost 250,000 pioneers set out from Independence, Missouri, in covered wagons on the Oregon Trail. Actually, most walked; the crude wagons and cruder "roads" made riding so uncomfortable. Men, women and children walked the plains, the badlands, the Rockies. They choked on dust, mired in mud. Some died. Some were born. They traveled 1,500 miles before they came to Flagstaff Hill just west of what is now the Idaho-Oregon border, the hill where sage plains lay behind them and the pine-clad Elkhorn Mountains beckoned beyond. At last! Oregon!

In this anniversary year, travelers can trace the Oregon Trail through five interpretive centers along the route that traverses Kansas, Nebraska, Wyoming and Idaho.

Through exhibits you can learn of life on the trail, mining, explorers and fur traders, natural history and Native American history. Or walk right into the past in the living history areas, where you can hunker near a fire at a wagon train encampment talking over the chances of an Indian raid. Or swap lies with a miner as he wipes sweat from his brow at a lode mine. At some points along the historic trail, you can even travel in the actual wagon ruts as part of a recreated trail ride.

My article "The Oregon Trail" will show Western families from the Mississippi to the West Coast how to participate in the myriad events organized for 1993, the 150th anniversary of the opening of the Oregon Trail. Through anecdotes about the variety of people who tramped the trail, I will dramatize how the Oregon Trail shaped the West. In a sidebar, I will outline the visitor centers and other travel services. And I will provide a selection of color photos. I see the piece especially suitable for the winter issue of 1993.

My work appears regularly in national and regional periodicals. I just finished two travel pieces: "Steens Scenes" will run shortly as a cover piece for the *Seattle Times* travel section, and an article on Ashland, Oregon, is the lead "Weekends" piece in the June issue of *Pacific Northwest.* I am currently on assignment with *Audubon* writing about the controversy in Hawaii over geothermal energy development in a rain forest.

I look forward to hearing from you again. Someday I'll offer the right idea! I hope this is it.

Sincerely,

Sally-Jo Bowman

There is really only one rule of query writing. That rule is this: "A good query must make the editor say 'Yes.' " (As the two letters above did.) *How* you follow that rule is what the first portion of this book is all about. I'll explain what a query is and what it isn't.

Before we get into that, you should understand *why* the query is.

Just for a moment, put yourself in an editor's shoes. (Being able to pretend that you are an editor is another excellent tool for the successful writer. But we'll save that discussion for later.) On your desk are three or four small stacks of paper, each one an article for the next issue. They are the typeset galleys of the pieces you edited last week. On top of them, the art director has just tossed the designs for the page layouts that she was supposed to deliver last week. Buried on the right corner of your desk are the quarterly budget projections, with a note from the accounting department asking for an explanation of why art costs are through the roof.

You turn your back to answer the ringing phone—it's the promotional people wanting to know where next year's editorial lineup is—and the mail clerk seizes the opportunity to slip the day's mail into your overflowing "in" basket. There they sit, twenty-five or thirty envelopes, only a couple of which are obviously press releases (and, therefore, candidates for quick trashing).

For the sake of argument, let's say that after sorting through the mail, you find ten query letters and ten full manuscripts. If you're the hard-hearted sort, you could return the latter ten unread; after all, your *Writer's Market* listing does say "Prefers queries." But that's not your style (you are the mythological editor with a heart of gold). So you're faced with a decision: Which do you attack first, the queries or the manuscripts?

Remember that the galleys still need proofing and the designs still await your okay, so you can't kick back for a relaxing hour of reading. But you need to spend some time looking over new material because a couple of holes remain in that lineup the promotion department keeps asking for. Perhaps today's mail holds that elusive fourth feature for September.

If you're like most editors, you're going to turn first to the query letters. The reason is fairly obvious: In the fifteen minutes before the art director comes back to talk cover concepts, you can likely consider all ten queries. You can read every word of each letter, even peruse the clips included by the best prospects. You can consider the author's sales pitch and make a decision—yes or no. (Your editorial assistant will later handle the dispensing of rejection notes.)

And what about the stack of manuscripts? Let's say you turn to it first. You still only have fifteen minutes—okay, twenty; the art director is always five minutes behind—but you still can't read every word and make it through all ten manuscripts. You grab the first. You read the first page. Midway through the second page, you start scanning. After page four, you skip to the end to see if there's anything surprising in the conclusion. Nope. You slap a Post-it note on the top, scribble "No" and move on. Five manuscripts into the pile and the art director is clearing her throat in the doorway.

Time is the major reason an editor prefers to review a query over a complete manuscript. And it's not just faster: It's a more efficient use of time. For her minutes, the editor reads a preview of the whole article—not just a dozen paragraphs at the top of a full-length manuscript. She can judge the depth and breadth of the writer's scope and how appropriate that approach is for her readers. She'll even have a better sense of who the writer is than she might get from a manuscript.

If the query were only a time-saver for editors, that would be enough for savvy freelancers to master the writing of this type of letter. But the query is similarly advantageous for writers.

You may have already encountered this scenario in your own writing, but if you haven't, feel free to envision the time you will. Yesterday was a fruitful day, and your reading and talking and brainstorming yielded a half dozen topics worthy of articles. Two of them will require some additional research to determine where they should go, but the other four came to you as ideas for specific magazines. Your files have yielded enough background material to support an intelligent proposal, but you'd need a week—at least—to dig up more current information, visit a site or two, and interview the proper sources before you could begin writing.

Here's your choice: Do you spend (collectively) a month or two pulling together facts and figures and quotes to write four articles that four editors may only partially read before they rush off to four art meetings? Or do you spend a couple days honing four sales pitches that will tell you whether any of these ideas will find a receptive market beyond your hard disk?

Again, the query is not only faster, but it's a more effective use of time. You have the opportunity to judge the marketplace before you commit yourself to the weeks of researching and writing. You have the opportunity to redraft the idea for other markets if the first editor you send it to isn't enthralled. You have the opportunity to build into your initial research the specific questions the editor tells you she wants answered in the article (rather than trying to revise the piece later). And you have the opportunity to judge this article's profitability by comparing the editor's payment to the time you'll need to research and write the article.

In the current psychobabble, I believe this is called a win/win situation. Both the editor and the writer enjoy the benefits of this particular sales tool. I know of no other trick of the trade that could be described as such. Everything else could more appropriately be termed win/whine.

Naturally, there are exceptions. Not every editor prefers query letters. Not every article can be queried. We'll look at these exceptions as we move along. But once you see how query letters work and learn how to write effective query letters of your own, you'll come to appreciate them as the most important sales tool you possess.

Before you wield this tool, however, you must first know who you're selling to and what you're selling. Once we've discovered how to lay the foundation for your queries, we can explore the writing itself.

CHAPTER TWO

Before You Send Anything . . .

When you meet an editor (like now, for instance), you can be certain of at least one piece of advice that she will pass along. In fact, this advice is shared so often that I've come to believe that there once must have been an editor's guild—the Sacred Order of St. Maxwell of Perkins—that required its members to offer this credo upon encountering a passing scribe. Max's guild has gone the way of the unicorn, but the mantra remains: "Know Your Market."

It's a simple phrase, too simple, perhaps, since every editor will also tell you that it is the most violated rule of freelancing. They see it violated in each day's mail, and often violated completely and totally. It's the manuscript entitled "Sex Life of Frogs" that shows up in *Writer's Digest*'s mailbag or the piece on "Mrs. Benedict Arnold" that stopped at *Woman's Day*. Less obviously off-base is the profile of novelist Tom Clancy intended for *Writer's Digest* that focused on the writer's relationship with Hollywood producers. Less obvious, perhaps, but it earned a rejection just as quickly as the amphibian sex guide. Neither author knew his market.

Given the number of writers who seem to ignore this most basic of the editors' exhortations, it would be reasonable to assume that it is a difficult task. To know a market must require a degree in journalism, at the least. Perhaps even a mastery of tectonic plate movements and an appreciation for astrology. Well, it does require an investment of time and some resources. Otherwise, it is no more difficult than reading critically.

You begin your exploration with a magazine in mind—a magazine you'd like to write for. Look at the publications you read regularly. Is there one you feel particularly drawn to, perhaps one that covers a topic on which you have something to say? And are you good enough for it? Is your writing's quality on par with what you usually see in this magazine's pages—could you legitimately expect to sell this publication's editor an article? This selection process calls for a healthy mixture of self-confidence and realism. I consider myself a competent writer, yet I don't routinely think of *The New Yorker* as a place to send my manuscripts. As a writer, I'm not in that league. (Yet.) When I'm judging potential markets to decide where to send my queries, I look for magazines where I can see my work fitting in. As you try to determine this, you might browse the biographical notes on the contributors in each issue. Are you in their league? If you're not now, are you really ready for the promotion?

Writers naturally gravitate to the most popular magazines—the ones they see on newsstands and on their neighbors' coffee tables. But so do the majority of other writers, including the experienced writers with numerous publication credits. Newer writers often do better if they seek out publications with lower profiles: The pay might not be as good, and your neighbors might not see your byline, but you'll also face significantly less competition from writers with higher profiles. Two types of publications that may be natural markets for you are those specific to your job and to your hobbies. Your experiences in these areas of your life probably give you several topics that other readers may want to know about and learn from.

To be fair, not every writer begins the query-writing process at this point. Many writers start with a topic and *then* cast about for a market appropriate to that idea. The system works for them and is no more wrong or right than my method. You may find that it works for you, either occasionally or routinely. But whichever comes first, idea or magazine, I believe you'll have more success as a freelancer if you pick out the specific aspects of your topic to write about while thinking of a specific magazine.

I'll try to explain this thought process by drawing an analogy to Christmas shopping. You could go to the mall and purchase a few items that look nice, are good bargains, or simply strike your fancy. As you wrap them, you tag each for a person on your Christmas list. Maybe that person will like the gift, but maybe not. If not, well . . . it's the thought that counts, right? But there was no thought. You bought the gifts because the price was right or the color was cute or you always wanted something like it yourself. You didn't buy it because it was perfect for Uncle Joe.

Meanwhile, your sister goes to the mall and assesses each item she sees against her gift list. Uncle Tim is into earth colors this year, so he'll appreciate this beige sweater. Uncle Wayne likes to let a bit of humor leak out around his conservative shell, so he'll love the white oxford shirt with the little Daffy Duck embroidered on the pocket. And Brittany will be glad to add this Polly Pocket house to her collection. It really doesn't matter if your sister saw the shirt first and then thought of Uncle Wayne or thought of Uncle Wayne and then set out to find a buttoned-down Loony Tunes item. Each gift was purchased with a specific—and appropriate—recipient in mind.

Picking a magazine, or magazines, to study is like drawing up your Christmas gift list before you head to the mall. Once you first understand this publication, you'll be better able to wrap up an idea that the editor will be happy to receive. You won't be sending out a query with the slim hope that the editor will like the same idea that appealed to you.

Once you've chosen a magazine to study, your first step is to read about the publication in a market guide, such as *Writer's Market*. These guides are designed with writers in mind and usually pass along a variety of pertinent information. Such information might include the editor's name, the types of articles needed, pay rates, time of payment, the rights purchased, tips for understanding the magazine's readers, and how much freelance writing is used (or whether it's not used—in which case you need to find a new publication).

The next step is to address a letter to the magazine's editorial department (you'll find the address listed in *Writer's Market*) and request a copy of the magazine's *writer's guidelines*. Creativity is neither expected nor prized in this letter; the following will work just fine:

Dear Editor:

I would like to receive a copy of your current writer's guidelines. An SASE is enclosed for your convenience.

Thank you,

Tough, huh?

(In the letter, *SASE* stands for "self-addressed, stamped envelope." You should include an SASE with every letter you send to an editor. This envelope should be a long business-size envelope—sometimes called a "#10"—unless a larger 9″ × 12″ or 10″ × 13″ envelope is needed to hold a magazine or a manuscript.)

What you'll receive in answer to your request varies. Occasionally you'll receive nothing: The request will either be lost or ignored, or the magazine's staff won't be polite enough to reply, "We ain't got 'em." (If they don't, *Writer's Market* will usually say so.) Sometimes you'll receive what might be charitably termed an information sheet. It reveals the magazine's general focus, its target audience, and a list of writing styles it doesn't wish to see (fiction and poetry most often head the list). While this information won't go much deeper than several superficial comments, it is vital. If an editor says she doesn't want to see something, she means it. Never say to yourself, "Well, that's just because she hasn't seen *my* poetry." There's hubris, and then there's the fast track to rejection. You're on the latter.

What you hope to receive in reply to your request for writer's guidelines is an information sheet—usually a page or two in length—that explains what the magazine is about, who it's written for, what types of articles the editors look for, and vital statistics regarding payment and such. It's sort of like a letter from the editor. Read it carefully.

Now you're ready to turn your attention to the magazine itself. Many magazines make available what are called *sample copies* to writers. That's a semi-exotic term for an issue of the magazine; there's nothing about these samples that is especially geared to freelancers. A few editors send out sample issues on request, others ask for an SASE, but most levy some charge. The cost is listed in *Writer's Market* and, unless *WM* says otherwise, you can include this request and a check when you ask for writer's guidelines.

If a magazine doesn't send sample issues, contact the circulation department and ask if you can order "back issues." Know that there is always a charge for these.

You may also obtain sample issues for some publications by buying them at the newsstand. A few cheaper ways are to ask neighbors and friends to save old magazines for you, swipe them from doctors' offices, or find a used-book store that also carries magazines. You could take up residence in the library's periodical room, but you'll appreciate having sample issues next to your typewriter as you write. I knew one freelancer who stopped each month at a local charter airline to pick up the magazines stocked on the planes for passengers. However you get them, my advice is to obtain between three and six issues published within the last twelve months.

Sleuthing the samples

Your ultimate goal in studying these sample issues will be to understand how the editor translates his writer's guidelines into flesh and pages. In them she may say she looks for "humor," but is she partial to lighthearted wit, exaggerated slapstick, collections of one-liners, or the subtlest of dry humor? She says she buys "relationship pieces," but what sorts of relationships are examined—dating, marital, friendships, business or some combination? Your goal is to gain a deeper understanding of the guidelines' basic points.

Begin your investigation with the "who": Who reads this magazine? How old are these readers? What sex are most of them? What sort of income do they bring home? What other characteristics bind them together?

The easiest place to discover the answers to these questions is in a magazine's advertisements. The advertising community expends considerable effort in pinpointing those publications whose readers are excellent prospects to buy their products—which is why ads for forty thousand dollar sports cars rarely show up in magazines read by middle-age, middle-income women.

For each ad you see, jot down a handful of words describing the consumers who are most likely to buy the product. That ad for a forty thousand dollar sports car might suggest this notation: "younger, high-income male, single." An ad for cookware: "young to middle-age women, home-oriented." Designer perfume: "women, higher-income." An investment fund: "Older men, higher income." (You should know that sexism is alive and well in advertising placement: Liquor, high-tech equipment and cars are usually advertised in men's magazines; home products, makeup, clothing and anything for children are pitched in magazines read by women.) Not every ad will suggest a narrowly drawn profile. Yet as you move through the magazine, you'll see a pattern emerge; there will be some common denominator in most of your descriptions. Maybe it's gender, maybe it's income, maybe it's age. Maybe it's some combination of factors. But however they're defined, these consumers are your target magazine's readers—and that makes them *your* target audience.

As you make this study, pay special attention to those ads that appear in issue after issue. Repeated insertions probably mean that the advertiser believes the magazine's readers are responding to the ad (that is, they're buying the product). This is particularly true with the small back-of-the-book ads; these advertisers generally live on tighter budgets and are not known for throwing new ad dollars after unsuccessful ones. What these ads tell you about the audience may be your best insights.

One way to confirm your reading of a magazine's audience is to lay your hands on the magazine's *media kit.* This is an informational package, assembled by a magazine's advertising staff, that is sent to potential advertisers. A media kit generally includes an issue of the magazine, a rate card (a price list for placing advertising space), testimonials from current advertisers, circulation figures and comparisons to competing magazines, an editorial calendar, and a variety of demographic information. This demographic information may be more than a simple portrait of the average reader's age, sex, marital status and income. Purchase patterns, travel habits, favorite hobbies, professions, educational background and more are regularly included. All of this will help you gain a deeper understanding for the audience you want to reach.

You'll also benefit from seeing the editorial calendar that may be included in the kit. The calendar tells advertisers what major themes the magazine expects to explore in the coming calendar year, including the topics of special issues. Knowing this information allows you to either avoid proposing these topics (if the issue date is within six months) or propose an appropriate article quickly (if the issue is more than six months away).

The problem with media kits is that most magazines won't send them to freelancers. They are expensive to produce (some might even be called glitzy, especially in highly competitive categories), so the advertising staff is anxious to make sure they only go to existing and potential buyers of ad space. And that's who you must pretend to be to acquire a media kit for your research. As acts of deception go, this is not a major production. Simply call the magazine's advertising department, tell whoever answers the phone that you're considering placing an advertisement and would like to see the magazine's media kit. If you're pressed for details, be vague. Say you're a consultant to a publisher that's thinking of advertising its books. Or whatever. (You're a writer. Be creative.) And should you receive a follow-up call from an advertising sales rep, well, shucks, your client decided to go with direct mail.

Even with the detailed demographic information of a media kit in hand, I still recommend doing the page-by-page advertising review. Your picture of who's reading this magazine will be even sharper as you see the specific products and lifestyles that attract these readers (and vice versa). You'll use this information just as advertiser's do: to match product and audience. The article idea that you'll try to sell in your query letter must be appropriate to this readership. It must tell them something they want to know. If you've been toying around with an idea on how to file for social security payments and you discover your target audience is only in its mid-twenties, think again.

As important as this reader profile will be to fulfilling the editor's exhortation to "Know your market," there's more work to do. Your next task is to decipher *why* these people read the magazine. What expectations do they come to it with?

It is a fact of modern publishing life that we live in an era of "service journalism"—that is, readers expect to be served in some fashion by the magazines they read. For the time I invest in *The Family Handyman*, I expect to be rewarded with tips for improving my home and property. After reading an article in *Runner's World*, I want to have learned how to run faster or improve my physical condition so I'll perform better next time I tie on my running shoes. The service angle isn't always so task-oriented—I consider myself served by the *Harper's Magazine* article that challenges my world view. And the *National Geographic* article that vicariously transports me to some remote destination I'll never visit. But nearly every reader expects some payback for the time he or she invests in an article. Your job is to discover what that expectation is so you can decide how you will fulfill that expectation as you prepare your idea and, later, your query letter.

Complementing the popularity of service journalism is the domination of the marketplace by a style of publication called the "special interest" magazine. Such publications focus on a specific topic; most often they'll name that interest in the title. *TV Guide*, for instance. Or *Parenting, Outside, Men's Health, The Artist's Magazine, Travel & Leisure*. A thorough thumbing of *Writer's Market* will expel any doubts you have regarding the abundance of special interest magazines. In fact, after a decade of compiling market information and studying the magazine industry, I've come to believe that any interest shared by three or more people very likely has a magazine devoted to it.

There are still general-interest magazines out there, of course—magazines that deal with most any subject that might interest readers. *Reader's Digest*, probably the world's best-known and most-read magazine, is the classic general-interest magazine. And there are the magazines I think of as hybrids—publications such as *Modern Maturity* or a few of the women's magazines that speak to a particular class of readers (retirees, women, young people) but otherwise take a general-interest approach. But no matter how you look at the market, the general-interest magazine is not as prevalent as it was in, say, the 1920s and 1930s—and even into the 1950s. In those times, magazines such as *Liberty* and *Collier's* and the old *Saturday Evening Post* played the role of general entertainer, a duty now filled by television. Today's readers look to magazines for depth of coverage on the topics that specifically interest them. Moms and dads look to *Parents* for help in toilet training Junior, skiers turn to *Ski* for help in finding the best resorts, and bodybuilders lift *Muscle & Fitness* to find a better biceps builder.

As a freelance writer looking to sell an article, it's not enough for you to simply know what a magazine's special interest is. You must also discover the magazine's "slant," which is its unique approach to presenting this special interest to readers.

Let me give you an example of how "slant" works—and why the successful freelancer must understand his target market's. At *Writer's Digest*, our special interest is writing. No secret there, right? It's in the title. As a result, we tend to receive queries and articles that deal with writing in any way, shape or form. Including: Lesson plans for teachers of creative writing. Reports on John Grisham's latest movie deals. Reviews of first novels. Essays bemoaning the success of *The Bridges of Madison County*, railing against the literary elite, and raising the banner of literacy campaigns—plus many more.

Now each of these pieces may be perfectly well written and may even come from authors with fine track records or worthy opinions. But none will sell to *Writer's Digest* because each misses our magazine's special slant. We are a magazine about *how to* write; our readers come to us to learn how to craft better short story openings and how to sell more articles and how to write stronger poems and how to lasso a Hollywood agent. If the article doesn't teach the reader something about being a writer, it won't work for us.

Within the office, we call it "The 4T Quality," which is shorthand for "Take To The Typewriter." (Disgustingly cute, I know. What's worse, I think I thought of it.) That means we look within each article for some piece of advice, some bit of knowledge that our readers will take back to their typewriters and do something better as a result—be it sell more articles or write more fascinating fiction. And we look for that in *every article*—be it a front-of-the-book short, a middle-of-the-book feature, or the last-page personal narrative.

And if your query doesn't show us that you understand *WD*'s slant, it won't succeed.

Discerning a magazine's slant may be as simple as reading the writer's guidelines. At *Writer's Digest* we explain our 4T quality right upfront. But for whatever lame reason, many editors don't. You may find a hint of the magazine's slant in the subhead that some magazines run on their covers or table of contents pages. *Complete Woman*, for instance, says it's "For All the Women You Are." *Condé Nast Traveler* carries the line "Truth in Travel." *Field & Stream* is "The Soul of the American Outdoorsman," and *Cooking Light* is "The Magazine of

Food and Fitness." All of these tell you something about how the editors view their publications and about the expectations they have for the articles they buy. But if the slant isn't spelled out in the guidelines or set in type on the cover, you must dive into the magazine and discover it. (Of course, even if you do find it in the writer's guidelines or on the cover, you'll want to closely study the magazine to see how the slant is carried through in the articles.)

There is no formula that will allow you to calculate an editor's editorial practices with mathematical precision. This is a process of reading closely, every page of every article and department, and of noting intentions and themes carried through a variety of article styles and topics. A good exercise is to ask, "Why are you here?" of every piece you encounter between the covers. And, "What benefit do you give readers?"

Note, too, the internal workings of each story. What are readers being told, what viewpoints are offered and in what tone? Are facts favored over opinions, and do the writers dig deeply into the topic or simply skim the surface of popular knowledge? Who's quoted, and how many speakers? How complex are the articles? Is the writing straightforward, or do the editors strain against the conventional? Are these "easy" reads, or do they demand readers' close attention?

After closely reading every article in several issues, you should be able to define the magazine's unique approach to presenting its specific topic to readers. And once you understand this slant, you'll know what expectations readers hold in their minds when they open each issue—and, therefore, what expectations your article must satisfy to be successful.

Because of the intensive investigation you had to undertake to determine your target publication's slant, the last step in studying this market will be fairly easy. You know what the readers' expectations are, now you must decipher how the editor fulfills those expectations.

Let's go back to *Writer's Digest*. The magazine's slant is there in the subhead—"Your Guide to Getting Published"—and you've determined that readers expect *WD* to teach them how to be better and more successful writers. The editors deliver on that expectation by publishing articles related to the writing of fiction, nonfiction, poetry and scripts. The range of article types is similarly narrow:

- how-to articles that examine and explain a specific technique of writing;
- profiles that feature a well-known writer explaining how he uses certain techniques;
- narratives that tell of one writer's experiences and the lesson about writing that he learned in the process; and
- informational reports on specific trends relevant to the writing industry or lifestyle, specific tools used by writers, and specific markets accessible by freelancers.

Not all magazines are as narrow as *Writer's Digest*, either in the subjects they cover or in the range of article types they use. One women's magazine's table of contents pages categorized that issue's articles under these major headings: relationships, love and sex, self-discovery, fashion and beauty, entertaining, health and diet, and business and money—plus a rundown of "regular features" that encompassed these topics plus current events, entertainment, humor, opinion and more. Obviously, that's a significantly more diverse playing field than at *Writer's Digest*. But knowing the magazine's slant will help you understand how this seemingly wild mishmash of subjects fits together into a unified whole that hundreds of thousands of women read monthly.

And that maybe—just maybe—you can write for. But first you must
  a. get an idea, and
  b. tailor it for a specific magazine.

That process is where you'll put all your newborn deductions to work—and lay the foundation for a successful query letter.

Finding ideas

If you haven't come to this realization already, let me put your mind at ease: There are no new ideas.

Some wit once said Homer wrote all the plots and Shakespeare did all the screenplays for Homer's plots, and everything since has just been variations on a theme. I take great comfort in that statement, even if the wit was talking fiction and we're dealing with nonfiction. What I find comforting is this: When I sit down to brainstorm, I know that I don't have to create something new. No one expects me to invent the wheel's replacement. Variations on the wheel will do just fine.

For instance, this book is not the first one ever written on the art and craft of writing query letters. It may not even be the tenth or the twentieth. But it is the first book on query writing to be part of a multibook series on the essential elements of nonfiction article writing. And it is the first book on query writing that includes my personal experiences and the lessons I've learned. Those elements were enough to make the editorial director of Writer's Digest Books say "Yes." And that's the only measure against which magazine (and book) ideas are held: Will it make an editor say "Yes"? If so, it's a good idea.

All the work you do in terms of studying a magazine is to help you identify the *themes* a particular magazine plays with. Your idea-generation sessions are the times when you come up with the variations on those particular themes that you wish to propose to the editor.

Where will these ideas come from? I could be glib and say they will come from wherever you find them. But that is also accurate. They will come from anywhere and everywhere. From what you see and what you hear; from what you carefully study and what you at first don't even realize you noticed. Your sources for ideas are limitless.

Most of them, however, will probably come either from the media or your own personal experience. You read about something that makes you think, "Gee, what if I looked at it from this angle?" Or, "I wonder if *Widgets Monthly* has heard about this new factory?" Or even, "Sheesh, did they get that all wrong!"

Art Spikol, who for many years wrote the Nonfiction column for *Writer's Digest*, once summed up the idea-generating process this way: "Most freelance writers are more like sponges than they are like supreme deities, so most of what they sell is not so much created as it is converted—absorbed, reprocessed, and released in another form."

Which means one day you see a mention in the Holiday Inn hotel directory about its in-hotel kids program, and then you see a newspaper ad for a new cruise ship specializing in families with kids, and then a friend tells you about the magazine Delta Air Lines sends his child each month and, presto, you're putting together a query letter about how the travel industry is catering to traveling families.

Some might call this serendipity, but not in my presence. This is what freelance writers do. They read hotel brochures and newspapers and magazines and notices pinned on bulletin boards, and (if they're really talented) pieces of paper sitting on the corner of the boss's desk. They listen more than they talk, and they ask questions of people who know about what's going on. And they eavesdrop shamelessly on others' conversations when nobody at their own tables knows more than they do.

They also look at themselves. Good freelancers tend to be as perceptive about the stuff within their own lives that will interest readers as they are about the stuff in the world around them. This doesn't mean they're writing little essays about the day their dog died or the problems they had with those silly moving men. It means that they consider their own lives as a source of ideas on par with the morning paper or that Holiday Inn directory.

"Write what you know" is ages-old freelancing advice. And what we know is tied up in what we've done. If we let them, our personal experiences can be an endless source of ideas for articles, stories on which you might say we have a "psychological copyright."

One writer I know, Michael Bugeja, believes the way to get a handle on such stories is to take "a broad, objective look at what you know."

To do this, wrote Bugeja in *Writer's Digest*:

> Jot down the "facts" of your life—the highs, lows, and turning points—the elements that distinguish your life from someone else's. Here are a few items from my list:
>
> I'm a first-generation American; I'm the oldest child; I married as a teenager; I am divorced; my father died of cancer; I remarried; my first baby was stillborn; I adopted an infant; I adapted as a father.

Go ahead and try Bugeja's exercise. Take five minutes and jot down the facts of your life. I'll wait.

Done? So what do you have—besides the outline for your obituary? You also have, depending on the number of entries on your list, the genesis of thirty, forty or more solid story ideas. But before you can write the query letter, you need to shape the ideas, give each a focus and a purpose. That purpose may be informational or it may be instructional (which is often called a "service" angle), but the purpose you find will almost always take the idea away from simply relating your experience.

How does this happen? When Bugeja wrote for United Press International, he drew on parts of his personal experience list for articles that were eventually accepted for the national UPI wire—the wire reporter's moral equivalent of a national magazine sale. In the following list, look how Bugeja took the raw experience and shaped it into a specific idea with a purpose that's evident just from the article's title.

Based on my list, I could write articles about:
- First-generation Americans of today, no longer European, but from such locales as Asia and the Middle East—"The Changing Faces of America's New First Generation"
- The responsibility and stress of the firstborn in family matters—"From Executor to Executive: Assuming the Family Business"
- Advice for teenage marriage success—"How Parents Can Help Their Children Make a Go of It"
- Offbeat divorce settlements—"If We Part, Who Gets the Football Tickets"
- The last chance for terminal cancer victims—"Remission: A Time to Make Up for Lost Time"
- The effect of stillborns on marriage—"Couples Most Likely to Divorce: How to Beat the Odds"
- Failed parenthood—"Adoptive Parents Who Return Their Children"

One technique you can apply in your brainstorming is to take each item on your list and ask, "What if?" Fiction writers are quite fond of this technique: Tom Clancy, for instance, traces the idea behind his first book, *The Hunt for Red October*, to a newspaper item about a Russian trawler that tried to flee to Sweden. The small boat was caught, but Clancy began to play "What if?" with the story: What if the boat hadn't been simply a trawler? What if the boat were a Soviet Navy ship? What if the boat couldn't be easily seen? What if it couldn't be heard? What if the Soviets told the Americans the defector was really a renegade with a nuclear arsenal? And so on and on and on—until Clancy had a plot line that fueled an international best-seller.

Luckily, fiction writers aren't the only ones allowed to play "What if?" (They already get to make up their facts; what more do they want?)

Let's play a bit of "What if?" using one of Bugeja's experiences. We'll say you adopted an infant. In reflecting on your situation, you begin to ask, "What if?" What if, after a few months, you realized you weren't cut out for parenthood, that you just couldn't handle it? Could you return the child? Has it ever happened? Or maybe your marriage was preceded by a long engagement. What if one of you never made it to the altar? What happens to the gifts? Could the no-show be sued for breach of contract? And what *does* happen to the ring? Or, as you reflect on a recent moving day, what if the moving men hadn't simply been obnoxious, but thieves, too? What sort of protection is out there? What safeguards are prudent?

Brainstorming—idea generation—is nothing more than extended sessions of questioning what you've seen and heard and done to see how you can make pieces fit together in intriguing ways. You could think of this process as working a jigsaw puzzle, except you don't have the picture on the box lid to guide your efforts. On the up side, of course, any two pieces may fit together. And even a single piece may form enough of the picture to inspire an article idea.

This is an intuitive process; there aren't many rules that govern it. But you can ask yourself three questions to help decide if the puzzle you've pieced together is worthy of further development. Assess your infant idea, and then ask yourself:

Is this topic interesting to me?

Let's say, for instance, that your idea centered on a trip you recently took. Did you find the trip interesting? Interesting enough to spend the necessary time researching, writing and marketing an article built around the destination or experience? How attracted are you to this idea, really? If you've taken up this idea purely because you believe the topic is "hot," think again. Such ideas rarely pay off, if for no other reason than the writer brings no imaginative fire to the resulting article. (Also, by the time you could deliver the manuscript, the idea will be frosty in the marketplace.) Especially in the early stages of your career, when you're developing your research and writing skills as you use them, make sure your topic is one you want to spend weeks, even months, pursuing.

Is there a reasonable chance that others will find my idea interesting, too?

Ideas that fail this test are what I like to call adventures in navel-gazing. You may find your own belly button fascinating, but I'm unlikely to share that interest. After all, I have one of my own. The place to contemplate the lint in your navel is a personal journal. For the magazine marketplace, select topics that others will invest in—both the purchase price of the magazine and the time it takes to read your piece. Tell us something we'd like to know. Take us somewhere we want to go. You must show us what you've found about your destination that is unique or compelling or attention-getting. Was your travel experience one that others would want to duplicate?

What can I say about this topic that hasn't been said previously or said in the manner I propose?

This is the question that too many writers fail to ask themselves. You may feel passionately about the abortion question, for instance. And we, too, may be interested in the topic. But it's unlikely that you can bring a viewpoint or episode to the forum that hasn't already been well aired in the many years of abortion debate. Or, on a less emotional subject, you may have rediscovered your inner child at Walt Disney World (see question #1) and feel fairly certain that others would want to duplicate the experience (see question #2), but what are you going to write about Walt Disney World that hasn't been written a hundred times before?

It can be tempting to answer that last one with some variant on this theme: "Well, *I've* not written about it. My voice will be what makes my piece unique." And for some writers, that's true. But let's face facts: Those writers have names that all by themselves attract readers and editors. Take, for example, Madonna. (Please?) By August 1994, her eccentricities and talents had been thrashed over in nearly every publication that could rub two columns of ink together. But when Norman Mailer chose to write about Madonna (or when he was asked to write about her—the genesis makes no difference), *Esquire* made the article its cover story. And the headline—"Mailer on Madonna"—let everyone know that this wasn't just another piece of Madonna bashing or Madonna beatification. It was two celebrity egos clashing in print.

And that's why *Esquire*'s editors made room for one more Madonna article.

Your article on Madonna, however, can't be billed the same way. Madonna's been written about to death and, unless you've been her bodyguard during her most recent concert tour or been granted an exclusive interview, your views won't earn you an assignment. But what about my earlier statements, when I said that although this book wasn't the first on writing query letters, part of what made it worthy of publication was *my* views on the topic? Am I contradicting myself? No. As editor of *Writer's Digest*, I have a credibility that may attract readers to this title. I'm no Norman Mailer, of course, but you take credibility in the amounts you can. And trust me, "Clark on Madonna" wouldn't attract a fraction of the reader interest generated by "Mailer on Madonna"; therefore (and thankfully), it wouldn't get the go-ahead from editors. Neither will your ruminations on how today's pop music groups are so much more [fill in the deprecation of choice] than the pop groups of your teen years. Nor your memory piece of the day you saw [fill in the name of your teen idol]. Nor any other piece that simply repeats, albeit in your own words, an article pitched by twenty other writers last week.

You must have something fresh to say.

Notice I didn't say "new." There are no new ideas, remember? The critical difference between new and fresh is that I can be fresh by examining an old subject from a different angle. The discussion isn't "new"—heck, I even may have lifted my angle from some report in a scientific journal that only sociologists read (properly attributed, of course). But to my audience of parents whose bachelor's degrees came in business and English (and who couldn't even name a sociology journal), I've delivered a fresh, insightful report that forced them to reexamine an old belief.

Being fresh is writing about the new hotels that opened last year at Walt Disney World. Being fresh is calling into question the perennial writing advice, "show, don't tell," through illustrations that demonstrate how great writers have at times told instead of shown. Being fresh is interviewing economists who believe that a large national deficit isn't necessarily a bad thing.

Sharpening the focus

Two crucial factors in deciding whether or not you have something fresh to say is knowing:

- who your audience will be, and
- what they've read before.

Remember what we said before about knowing the market? This is where your work pays off. By studying the market you learn who your audience is. You will also have seen, firsthand, how the magazine in question covers particular topics—or doesn't cover them, which isn't necessarily the good news it may seem. From this accumulated knowledge you can make assumptions about what the average readers of this magazine know about, say, the Internet or marital relationships or mutual funds. You can then compare that level of knowledge to your idea: Will you be telling them something they already know, would like to know, or don't care to know?

Notice that I did not include "need to know" among the options. That's because it's already represented in my list by "don't care to know." There may be many topics that readers of a particular magazine might truly *need* to know. But if they don't *want* to know it, they won't stop to read your article. (That's if they even get the chance. The editor likely knows her audience's distaste for your topic and will reject it before the story can be passed over by her readers.) The writer's challenge in this case is to seek out a way to make the topic, for lack of a more delicate term, "sexy." You must make this information desirable. If you know that readers need to know how to complete an IRS form, but you also know that few readers would willingly submit to a line-by-line instruction sheet, then your task is to make the topic appealing. Something like, "Fifteen Common Tax Form Errors That Are Costing You $$." Even the most taxaphobic reader will grab that line off the newsstand.

What I did in that example was reduce an article idea to a single line, one that could be printed on the cover of a magazine to entice readers. (In the industry we call them "cover lines." We are a clever bunch, aren't we?) This reduction may strike some as simplistic, but envisioning your idea as a cover line is an excellent way to get a grip on the idea you're shaping. That grabber of a line can also double as the working title for your story, the umbrella under which everything else must fit. For instance, if you were outlining what you'd say in a story titled "Fifteen Common Tax Form Errors That Are Costing You $$," you'd instantly know that a history of the 1040A form lay outside the area covered by that headline. So you'd leave it for another article.

You can also look at this cover line and ask yourself, "Will my target audience be attracted to this teaser?" This comes back to knowing your audience. If your audience is CPAs, they likely know all fifteen tax form errors—and another thirty to boot. Your line wouldn't be fresh; you'd need to continue shaping the idea to find an angle that would be appealing to your target market.

Of course, what's old news to one group of readers might be fresh as a high-school Romeo to another group. CPAs might know the tax form errors, but the average homeowner might not. Sometimes you only have to move an idea from one market to another to find a good fit.

For an active freelancer, this shuffling of idea glimmers among potential markets is standard operating procedure. And it's a part of the freelancing process that rewards writers who read a variety of magazines. To break in with a magazine, you must know it intimately. And to know a magazine intimately, nothing beats reading it regularly. If there's a magazine you really want to break into, stick a crowbar in your wallet and subscribe to it. (Provided you make an effort to sell there and are making at least some money freelancing, the cost is tax deductible.)

It may help you develop your abilities to match glimmers to magazines by imagining yourself to be a "field editor" for the magazine. Your "job" will be to seek article ideas for the publications that most interest you.

"Field editor" is a term that betrays my newspaper roots. In days gone by, before wire services became newspapers' eyes and pens in the hinterlands, a newspaper would hire a writer who lived beyond its territory to send in periodic reports about what was happening where he was. These writers went by a variety of names, including "correspondent" and "field editor." But they couldn't write about just anything. They were charged with sending in reports about local activities, personalities and events that would be of interest to the newspaper's hometown readers. Say, for instance, that you were a correspondent in the employ of a New York newspaper and you lived in—and wrote about for that paper—Cincinnati. Now the major controversy in Cincinnati at that time might have been the frequent appearance of live pigs in the street, escapees from the nearby slaughterhouses. But as a correspondent for a New York newspaper, you would know that New Yorkers would have no interest in such a swine state of affairs. *Your* readers would be more interested in the railroad the city was building to its south with the intent of opening up a north-south lane of commerce that could compete with the Mississippi River packets. Such an alternative, said its proponents, would cut shipping costs dramatically—news that consumers and investors back in New York would be eager to hear.

Modern-day freelancers can apply the same technique—with or without the regionalism. Sure, if you want to write for *Outside* magazine, you can pay close attention to local environmental controversies or recreational areas in the hopes of contributing an item that might have escaped the notice of *Outside*'s faraway editors. But just as those editors aren't reading the same newspapers or hiking in the same foothills as you, they also haven't had your unique life experiences or eavesdropped on the commuters you did last week. The article idea that was born from the coming together of that overheard conversation and a long-ago experience may have no regional angle at all, but it still could only have come from your "field office."

As you sit in this office brainstorming, review the articles that have appeared over the past several issues. Now, play editor. Put yourself in her shoes. What topics would you run next? What would be your dream article?

Chances are, you'd look for more of what you've been doing. Remember the Hollywood adage, "The same, only different"? Editors at successful magazines see what's working with the audience and then go looking for pieces that are similar to those—interesting variations on the theme, you might say. (At magazines where circulation and advertising numbers are falling, it's more like, "I'll try anything!") As you imagine yourself to be a field editor, you should be coming up with variations on the themes and topics that you're seeing each month in the magazine, without actually repeating what's already appeared.

Nothing leaves a worse impression on an editor than querying an article that appeared in the magazine within the last six months. It doesn't just imply that you haven't studied the market, it goes into court and swears to that fact.

(A proviso to the no-repeats rule: If you go back far enough—say, more than three years—you may find old articles on topics that could be updated, run through your personal viewpoint, and sold to the market again. Magazine readerships "turn over" every few years—as do the editors—so magazines can safely repeat topics. If you decide to pour some old wine into a new bottle, you must still write a new, original article with new sources and updated information. But you may need to revise the hook only slightly.)

Curiously enough, many writers—inexperienced *and* experienced—overlook the magazine's core subject matter when proposing topics. They send queries that nibble at the corners of the magazine's target, rather than shoot an idea straight down the middle. At *Writer's Digest*, for instance, we routinely see queries on such how-to sidelights as writing restaurant reviews or organizing your correspondence files or breaking into the motorcycle magazines. We call them "tangential"; it's one of the options on our check-off rejection letter. Yet we never see enough proposals for our meat and potato topics: how to write dialogue, for instance, or how to create effective transitions, or even how to organize your articles. Organize your filing cabinet? Sure. But nothing on organizing stories. It's a syndrome *Writer's Digest* columnist David Fryxell once described this way: "Query writers keep choosing to aim for the eye of a needle rather than a wide-open garage door."

Study your target markets, then put yourself into the editor's chair. Go so far as to draw up a list of stories that you'd put into the table of contents over the next couple of months. (And, remember, readers shouldn't notice a change in direction. That risks a drop in subscription renewals.) Now, slip back into your field office and take a look at that list; which of those articles could you write?

Part of the beauty of this arrangement is that the staff members at your target magazines won't ever know that you've set yourself up as a field editor. You do this on your own, by simply reading the publication (or publications; you can take on as many field editorships as you wish) and then sifting all your observations through a sieve specially designed to catch those nuggets that might be shaped into something for one of your "clients." (If you long for a more tangible sign of your "special" relationship, buy a T-shirt or ball cap emblazoned with the magazine's logo; nearly everyone sells something of the sort these days. In fact, *Outside* even sells hats that say "Field Staff.")

It should go without saying that you can't pass yourself off as a field editor to public relations people or government officials or anyone else. It should, but I feel better saying it anyway.

Fashioning the idea's hook

Once your mental sieve snares an idea that's appropriate to your target market, you still aren't ready to begin writing a query. Just as a gem cutter must cut and polish a raw gemstone before it can be placed in a jeweler's display case, you must polish and cut your raw idea.

Generally, the ideas that first strike us are big pictures. Yes, you've identified the topic as being ripe for a particular market. But you must still find an angle into this subject that's compatible with the magazine's slant. This angle is often called the "hook"; that is, it's the aspect of your idea that will snare readers (starting with the editor) and pull them into your article.

The hook is, quite simply, the thing that turns an interesting subject into a salable story idea. Any number of magazines might consider an informational piece on vitamin E or a collection of workout tips or advice for handling stress. These are topics of interest to many people, but each requires a spin that will intrigue your target market's specific audience. Here are the hooks each topic got at *Men's Health*: "The *One* Vitamin Every Man Needs," "Workout Secrets for Faster Results," "Stay Focused: How to Blow Off the Ten Worst Male Stressors."

And like so much of this creative process, there are no formulae for divining a winning hook. But here are a few questions to ask as you work on your gemstone.

What piece of this subject is specific to my target market's readers?

Look at the notes you made while studying your target market's advertising. Who's reading this magazine, and what—specifically— would these people want to know about the topic you've identified?

"Stress" is one of those big picture ideas. It's large enough to have comfortably accommodated a best-seller list full of books, yet it is the raw idea behind articles that regularly show up in table of contents pages. For example, writer Todd Balf polished up the "stress" chestnut for *Men's Health* by posting a "for men only" sign on the topic. His "Get Past Tense" looked at stress from a man's point of view; as the subhead put it: "The top ten male stressors from job worries to trouble on the home front. How to spot them and how to squelch them." Balf doesn't say his ten stressors apply *only* to men (women experience stress related to both job and marriage, too). But he hooked *Men's Health*'s readers with a promise to look at these stressors, and their cures, through a man's eyes.

What's new with this topic?

Yes, I said there are no new ideas. But life evolves and, as it does, technology and research and good ole ingenuity advance humankind's various abilities. To use a fiction analogy, "man versus machine" was among those themes first written up by Homer and his peers. But in the dawning of computers, many science fiction writers recognized they could expand the genre by pitting man against these newfangled machines. Likewise, for every step we take forward, article writers have opportunities to update readers. Remember that flood of stories about the Internet in 1994? They were essentially no different from the flood of stories fifteen years ago on personal computers. They simply looked at the new technology of the moment from a point of view appropriate to the audience. If you can pick up on a trend early enough, you too can be part of these periodic waves. (It seems a new one sweeps through every month or so.)

What hasn't been written about this topic?

If this sounds remarkably similar to the discussion of "fresh" ideas above, you're right. As you research ideas, look for those angles left underdeveloped by other writers. Perhaps your personal experience gives you an insight others might not have—or have not written about. Two articles on the same topic stick in my mind as examples of this idea. When I was a college student, the national debate over abortion was young, and I remember being moved by a *New York Times* op-

ed essay written by a woman who was haunted by her long-ago decision to abort a pregnancy. It was the first article of that kind that I'd
seen. Five years later this woman's article probably would have gone
unpublished because it had by then been done repeatedly. Yet there
was room in the topic for a first-person narrative written for *McCall's*
by a woman who wrestled with the abortion question when a doctor
said (mistakenly, it later turned out) that her unborn child would have
serious health problems. The twist that took this article beyond all the
previous abortion-issue pieces: The woman was a former nun.

When you look at what all the other writers are saying on a topic,
see if the flip side is getting its due. The article that questioned the
"show, don't tell" dictum of writing is a contrarian view that I bought
for *Writer's Digest*. An *Outside* magazine columnist took a similar
approach when he suggested the no-impact movement among campers
might be going to ridiculous extremes.

Does the magazine's slant dictate my hook?

For a "how-to" magazine such as *Writer's Digest*, an article's hook
may be almost preordained. What will snare me—and my readers—is
a promise to teach new writers how to master a particular writing
or marketing technique ("How to Write Effective Query Letters," for
instance—and I think I know who will write it). Even in the article
that took a new look at "show, don't tell," the writer's hook included
a promise to reveal the secrets of effective "telling." For such magazines, the most challenging creative question in crafting ideas may
come as you decide how much or how little of the topic to tackle.

In fashioning your hook, you must consider how much of the topic
you can tackle within the confines of your article. In the best of all
worlds, you could write as many words as needed to cover your topic.
You could cast a wide net, pulling in all sorts of tangents, while delving
into every point as deeply as you wished. But magazine articles can
only hold a limited number of words, usually no more than 3,000
words. In today's market, the word count may be as few as 1,000.
And those are feature lengths. Articles slated for a specific department
get even less space, sometimes as few as 300 words. Occasionally you
may wonder if you're writing an article or just a long filler item.

Trimming your idea means finding the meat of your hook while keeping one eye on your target market. Your hook, for instance, may demand a 3,000-word treatment. But if your market never carries an article that exceeds 2,000 words, you need to get out the pruning shears and reshape your hook. Your challenge is to determine how much ground you can cover and how deep you can till that acreage. I find it helpful to picture myself drawing a box around the topic. If I draw a wide box, then I can't extend it very deep into the topic without running over the target market's preferred article length. Conversely, the deeper I dig, the less breadth my article can afford.

For an example, consider Todd Balf's article on the top ten male stressors. This is a longer piece (by today's standards): It runs about 2,500 words. That's the size of the box Balf could draw around his topic. For argument's sake, we'll say Balf knew his hook would be a list of those stressors that attack men especially hard. But how many? If he drew the box wide enough to encompass a hundred stressors, each item would get about 25 words. That's a list with minimal explanation, let alone depth or helpfulness. Even a box wide enough to cover twenty-five items couldn't also allow enough depth to describe the stressor and tell how to make it go away—the latter being the service element essential to *Men's Health*. To accomplish both goals would require somewhere between 150 and 300 words per stressor, so Balf could only stretch the article's box over ten items.

How did Balf know how many words he'd need to cover each of his stressors? Unfortunately, that's the sort of guesstimate a writer can only make out of his past experience. Or when an editor tells you, "Give me a list of ten items, and wrap the piece up in 2,500 words." Necessity really is the mother of invention.

Six types of articles

As you determine your hook, you'll benefit from deciding what type of article the piece will be. The list that follows offers six of the most common styles of articles; you are probably familiar with these types, but I've named a real-life example of each to help you visualize them. With each type, I offer the start of a sentence that will help you encapsulate your idea. If you can't put your hook into one of these sentences, or one similar to them, your idea is still too unformed to begin your query letter. You must continue to polish and cut it.

• The "think" piece. ("Have you ever considered . . .") Also called an "essay," the think piece is among the harder types to carry off. While you must work from a solid base of research, the article depends on the quality of your own thoughts. As such, you need a penetrating mind and the ability to see what has previously been unseen in a topic that's important to the audience. That last element is crucial; editors see far too many essays of navel-gazing. Your insights must connect to a universal—or, at least, an audience-wide—concern. Examples: "The Waiting Game" (subhead: "We've earned the right to stride fearlessly about a man's world—and to do so alone. But is this really what we want?") in *Healthy Woman*; "You Are What You Shoot" (subhead: "Let's stop calling the gun issue a debate over constitutional rights; it's a collision of cultures") in *GQ*.

• The information piece. ("Did you know that . . ." or "Have you heard about . . .") This is an article built on telling readers about some topic. List articles, behind-the-scenes visits and exposés fall into this category. Examples: "America Goes Stir (Fry) Crazy" in *Smithsonian*; "All About All-Inclusives" in *Caribbean Travel & Life Magazine*.

• The how-to article. ("Here's how to . . .") Often written in a step-by-step progression, this piece explains how readers can complete some task themselves. Examples: "Be a Layer Player" (subhead: "How to piece together a comfortable outfit for any cold-weather condition") in *Bicycling*; "Rewire Your Hot Buttons" in *New Woman*.

• The travel article. ("Have you ever visited . . .") This is a piece that reveals to readers a specific destination. The form can be similar to either an information piece or a how-to article, but the travel aspect is what defines this article. Examples: "England's Wildest Shore" in *Condé Nast Traveler*; "The Great Escapes" (subhead: "From St. Vincent to the Sierras, twelve quick cures for cabin fever") in *Men's Journal*.

• The personality profile. ("Have you met . . .") These articles tell readers about nearly any aspect of an individual's life. Q&A interviews fall into this category as well. Examples: "The Present-Minded Professor" (subhead: "Why are your kids' teachers watching this man so closely—and how's he going to spend $385 million to reform our nation's schools?") in *Child*; "Why Isn't Barry Bonds Willie Mays?" in *GQ*.

• The personal experience piece. ("Have I ever told you about the time . . .") Marketing an article that only recounts an experience can be difficult. You'll have more luck using a personal experience as a jumping off point for framing one of the other five types. Examples: "I Lost My Husband to a Cult" in *Redbook*; "Memoirs of a Once Decadent Girl" in *Cosmopolitan*.

Brainstorming is not among writing's easiest tasks—at least for me. And the number of writers who are routinely asked, "Where do you get your ideas?" testifies that their interrogators want answers too. But any editor will tell you that she has no problem related to the quantity of ideas she receives. Her concern is quality—no one sees enough good ideas. The solution? "Know your market." The best query letters are born out of the time you spend studying your target magazines and using that information to hone the hook you'll use to snag a place in those pages.

When that's ready, it's time to put words on paper.

CHAPTER THREE

Approaching the Query Letter

When you sit down to write a query letter, the most important fact to remember is that your fitness for this assignment will be judged by the piece of writing you place into the envelope. Over the years, I've heard and used many intriguing analogies: The query letter is a handshake, an application for employment, a singles' club pickup line. All are valid, but also somewhat short of the mark.

When you meet someone for the first time, you will likely introduce yourself and shake hands. Many business people take the measure of a person through this ritual. A firm, dry handshake is supposed to indicate a self-confident, straightforward individual—a person who's not afraid to be in this particular situation. A query letter must convey the same attitude. As a writer, you don't want to appear to be in water over your head. Your letter must convey confidence in your idea, confidence in your talent, and confidence in your ability to "fit in" with the other authors appearing in the magazine's pages.

When an employer reviews an application for employment, he or she wants evidence of your appropriateness for the open position. What's your background, what are your credentials, and why are you someone I should be interested in? Those are questions your query letter must also answer.

And what about the query letter as pickup line? The most successful barroom Romeos are the ones who are able to establish an immediate connection. They aren't the hapless multitudes muttering, "What's your sign, baby?" Their approach is unique—or at least it sounds unique. It may be something about what the woman is wearing or about her appearance or about the surroundings. Wherever the line springs from, it is not generic. The woman knows that it has been created just for her. And you must approach the seduction of magazine editors in the same fashion.

So how can this book exist? If each letter must be a unique creation, constructed solely for a particular idea for a particular magazine, how can I promise to teach you what to say?

The lessons that follow will introduce you to strategies and principles. I will not be putting words in your fingers anymore than an evening workshop in "How to Meet Members of the Opposite Sex" can put an appropriate pickup line in your mouth. But in learning the rudiments of the form, you'll have a framework on which to base your own letters. In this chapter and the ones that follow, we'll also look at a variety of successful query letters to see how their authors applied these strategies and principles to win assignments.

I offer these samples as models, not templates. Many years ago, *Writer's Digest* ran an article by Lisa Collier Cool on writing query letters. That article included, as an illustration, a copy of the query letter Cool had sent us proposing this particular feature. Shortly after that issue appeared on the newsstands, we began to notice a certain "sameness" in the query letters appearing in the *Writer's Digest* slush pile. We eventually recognized that sameness as near carbon copies of Cool's letter—different ideas, but the same tone and (in many cases) the same words. This was particularly noticeable in the letters' closings, which mimicked Cool's uncommon "I look forward to your reaction." It's inclusion in everyone else's letter was an indication that the sender was perhaps something less than an original thinker.

So I warn you now: This is not a cookbook. You cannot follow another writer's "recipe" and produce a query letter that sells. As a cook, I can produce an apple pie identical to the one produced by the authors of *Joy of Cooking* because the people seated at my table have likely not dined with those authors. And, though a chef will cringe at this statement, one apple pie is not much different from every other apple pie. But a magazine article is unique; an article examining, say, today's political currents will be very different if it is written for *The New Republic* than if it is written for *National Review*. And yet still different if it is written for *Reader's Digest*, and yet again for *The New Yorker*.

This individuality is what editors look for in determining your fitness for an assignment. Every editor—especially editors of the largest-circulation magazines—receives query letters that have all the uniqueness of a "Dear Occupant" letter. And every editor learns to recognize such letters as clearly as she sees a flashing "danger" beacon on the highway. Your task as a freelance writer is to direct each query letter to a specific editor and to make sure the editor recognizes this effort. This goal is appropriate even if you are submitting a simultaneous query—that is, if you are sending the same idea to more than one magazine. Although editors' prejudices against this practice are fading, editors still insist that writers tailor their ideas to the editor's magazine. To mail merge a list of potential buyers to a generic query letter is certainly time efficient, but the results will rarely pay off even that minimal investment.

Adopting the right tone

One description of a query letter that I'm not fond of is to call the query "a business letter." The description is not inaccurate (I love how double negatives carry that connotation of "true—but not right"); a query letter is written by one businessperson (the freelancer) to another (the editor) in the hopes of creating a business relationship (the contracting for and sale of a manuscript). But people do not generally think of business letters as stylish showcases of writing—or even *interesting* presentations of writing. Thinking of a query letter as a business letter often leads to letters that begin:

> Dear Editor:
> Please find enclosed an idea that I hope you'll find suitable for your magazine. . . .

And such letters nearly always lead to SASEs bearing rejection slips.

Tied up in this matter are two qualities that concern all writers: style and tone. Now "style" is one of those concepts that I believe has been ruined by English professors and literary critics. After a lifetime of literature courses, we all know that Hemingway had style, that Fitzgerald had style, and—if you went to school in the South—that Faulkner had style. Beyond that, the professors suggest, no one else has style. Especially you there, in the fourth row.

I'm exaggerating, of course, but the notion that you don't possess a personal writing style is sheer nonsense. We all have "style," which is nothing more than the expression of your voice on paper. Hemingway, Fitzgerald and Faulkner may have written in distinctive styles, recognizable styles, but that is because each of them worked first to recognize and develop his voice at the keyboard and then to trust it in his writing. Your own style may be raw and unrefined, but you still have one, and it is one of the qualities an editor will look for in your query letters.

I've found that the editors who are most concerned with voice are those at the largest, most prestigious publications. That's logical; their magazines are the markets that receive the most submissions, so these editors have the luxury of holding out for the very best writers. In fact, they often consider voice to be the crucial element in determining whether a writer wins an assignment. And that's part of the reason why it's hard for a newer writer, a writer whose voice may still be rough and uncertain, to make a sale in the most prestigious markets. The editors prefer to go with the finely tuned writing.

How do you reach this echelon? The answer is simple—at least simple to point out: You must practice. You can read all of Hemingway's and Fitzgerald's and Faulkner's works—as well as all the other classics and nonclassics; you can read all the how-to-write books ever published; you can even debate the elements of "voice" until the barroom tap runs dry. But if you never pick up a pen or position your fingers on the keyboard of a typewriter or word processor, you will never develop your writing voice. There is no substitute for writing. The writer who is serious about developing his writing voice is the writer who puts words on paper every day. He may do so in a journal. He may put them down in letters to his mother. He may pen the most narrative shopping lists ever seen. And none may ever be seen by an editor. But the words that are meant for an editor's eyes will be voiced with more self-confidence because of those daily practice sessions.

The other quality at work in the writing of a query letter is "tone," which is a matter separate from voice. A writer's voice can take on many tones—many complexions, you might say. You can hear tone demonstrated in the work of a singer. One of my favorites is Mandy Patinkin. Obviously, Patinkin has just one voice. Yet he can manipulate that voice to render the wonder-filled reflection of "I Remember," the driving lament of "Brother Can You Spare a Dime," and the tender romance of "Younger Than Springtime." And a dozen more moods, depending on the demands of a particular song. All are different from each other, yet all share Patinkin's distinctive voice.

Just as a singer can use dynamics and phrasing and tempo and rhythms to achieve a specific effect, a writer can color the tone of his work. The tone of a written piece can be sentimental or unsparing, smooth or rough, florid or spare, friendly or detached, inviting or assaulting—all determined by a battery of elements including everything from word choice to sentence length to structure. When you write for a magazine—beginning with the query letter—part of the challenge is to fit your piece within the magazine's overall tone. That may be scholarly or irreverent or homespun or technical; your study of the market will tell you which.

When I said that I'm not fond of referring to query letters as business letters, I was especially thinking of tone. Instead of a business letter, think instead of writing a personal letter to an acquaintance. Don't think close friend, as close friends often share a shorthand that allows them to write almost in sentence fragments and still be completely understood by the reader. You likely don't have that relationship with an editor. (And even if your best pal is an editor, you're queries should still be complete enough for other staff editors to understand your proposal.) The tone required in a query letter would be more akin to the tone you'd use with an acquaintance, or perhaps with a relative outside your immediate family. Approach the editor as one with whom you can be yourself, one who appreciates your sensibilities and warmth.

The editor receiving this letter will not, of course, have the same appreciation of your personality as someone you know personally. But your personality is what you want the letter to convey. You want the editor who reads your letter to recognize that you, first of all, *have* a personality. Second, you want the editor to see that you are a writer who can be trusted to make the English language do his bidding.

How do you achieve this effect in a letter to someone you've never met? First, recognize that you know this editor better than you might think. If you've been studying the market carefully over a period of several issues, you have likely inferred at least a few character traits about the editor. This was driven home to me many years ago at a writers' conference. A woman attending my session had stopped to ask me some questions about *Writer's Digest*. As we talked, she said something along the lines of "I'll bet the editor [who was not me at the time] has a pretty good sense of humor."

"Yes he does," I replied. "But how did you know that?"

"From the subheads in the magazine," she answered. "I figured anyone who would write those puns had to have a good sense of humor."

Clearly, this was a freelancer who had a thorough knowledge of the magazine.

You may also establish a link with the editor by using a line or two of your letter to comment on something you know about the editor. Editors who regularly write some sort of "Letter From the Editor" column often reveal their personal interests or life events. You might learn from reading this page that you share an interest in a particular sport, hail from the same part of the country, or attended the same university. You should feel free to mention such shared interests in your query letter, especially if it has some relevance to the article you're proposing. "I remembered reading in your column about your interest in skiing. So I thought of your magazine as the best home for my article, 'Five Best Undiscovered Ski Resorts of the Rockies.' "

You might also comment on a recent accomplishment by the editor or the magazine. Congratulate the editor on a recent promotion, for instance, or some prize the magazine recently won. Sure, this is flattery—and most editors will recognize it as such. They will also know whether the flattery is genuine or not. Everyone likes to be recognized for what she does, and editors are no different. But no one likes to feel used. No editor is going to be softened by such effusive fawning as this: "No wonder you were chosen as editor! Your recent articles in the magazine have revolutionized our industry in a way not seen since

Tom Wolfe created New Journalism." But something along the lines of "I've long appreciated the information I've picked up in your articles, so I was pleased to learn you recently took home the National Magazine Award for Personal Service. I believe that the article I've proposed will continue that tradition." Or, "I thought the structure you used in your September article on working with a remodeling contractor worked quite well for conveying a lot of information. I think a similar structure would be appropriate for my proposed piece on how to select the best financing plan."

Done well, a brief mention of some shared interest or recent accomplishment by the editor helps your letter stand out from the other faceless queries. And when coupled with an idea accurately targeted to the magazine's readers, it can further demonstrate your familiarity with the market.

There are other ways to achieve a friendly tone in your letters. Imagine you are describing your idea to a friend; use that sort of language in your letter. Long sentences packed with multiple thoughts are harder to comprehend on first reading than shorter, single-thought sentences. Favor simpler words, too; don't say *conflagration* when *fire* will do just fine, thank you. Write *use* instead of *utilize*, *meet* instead of *interface with*. Use jargon sparingly, unless it's appropriate to the market and the nature of your letter. One very simple step toward friendlier prose is to use contractions. To my ear, "I don't anticipate a problem" sounds far more inviting than "I do not anticipate a problem." And if I ask you, "Don't you agree?" you'll feel more comfortable giving me an answer than if I ask, "Do you not agree?" It's all in the tone.

If you're a writer who feels comfortable dropping in a bit of humor, feel free to lighten the overall tone of your letter. A humorous turn of phrase or anecdote can help overcome an editor's initial reserve—just as a good chuckle does in face-to-face first meetings. James Morgan once wrote in *WD* about a query letter he'd received while he was articles editor at *Playboy* magazine. "I *knew* I liked this guy when he typed his letter almost to the bottom of the first page, and when I turned to page 2, I found this: 'I'll discuss how much of a margin to leave at the bottom of the first page of a query letter.' "

Not every writer would feel comfortable putting such an aside into a letter. Nor would every writer be able to pull it off as well as Morgan's correspondent. And, alas, not every editor would appreciate it as much as Morgan. But I think most do, and I like to call upon it in my own letters. Here's a portion of one I sent to a video magazine. The idea didn't sell, but the editor's reply included two lines freelancers love to hear: "I like your style" and "Please try again." Here was an editor who obviously appreciated the fine (?) art of the running gag.

> Forget Sam Shepard. Forget Dennis Quaid and Scott Glenn. They may have had *The Right Stuff*, but they haven't shown "the write stuff." (Well, maybe Shepard. But not on screen.) Look instead to William Hurt (*The Accidental Tourist*), Tom Selleck (*Her Alibi*), Nick Nolte (*Weeds*), Brian Dennehy (*BestSeller*), Alan Alda (*Sweet Liberty*), Matthew Broderick (*Brighton Beach Memoirs*, et al.), and, of course, Kathleen Turner (*Romancing the Stone*).
>
> In the past five years or so, the "write stuff" has been hot stuff as far as Hollywood is concerned. Writers are turning up (ready for this one?) left and write in movies, from leading players (see *Reds* and *Barfly*) to supporting characters (see Jeff Goldblum in *The Big Chill*).
>
> I've identified three dozen recent videotapes that feature writers among the movie's characters. I'll highlight the best—up to and including James Earl Jones's J.D. Salinger imitation in *Field of Dreams*—in a 1,500-word roundup that I have to call "The Write Stuff" just so I can get that pun out of my system. As managing editor of *Writer's Digest* magazine, it comes to mind a lot.
>
> I've enclosed a couple clips of my work at *Writer's Digest* to demonstrate my writeness (ouch) for this assignment. . . .

Humor is a delicate element. The topic of your query letter may be one that doesn't lend itself to humor, nor will the character of every magazine suggest that a chuckle would be welcomed. Even where humor is appropriate, know that light touches can go a very long way. You aren't writing a stand-up routine, after all. I probably carried it as far as a writer should in the letter above—and even then the chuckles grew out of a single gag. Never risk knocking your idea out of the editor's spotlight for the sake of a chuckle. All you want is to convey that you are a writer who comes complete with a sense of humor.

Beyond a friendly tone, you want to approach the editor with confidence. Remember my comparison of the query letter to an application for employment? If you were hiring someone to fill a position, would you favor the applicant who sat up straight, answered questions with a steady voice, and described himself as a can-do sort of employee? Or would you take on the applicant who appeared to be swallowed up by the chair, whose voice seemed to come through a handkerchief, and who responded to the job description with a hesitant, "Well, I think I can do all that"?

One thing a writer can't do in a query letter is doubt himself. If you don't believe you can pull off the assignment, either forget it completely or write a brief note to the editor offering the suggestion as "something you might consider assigning to one of your writers." (As an editor, I sometimes get notes like this from readers. "I'm pretty confused by this whole viewpoint technique. I'd love to see an article on it sometime." I want to kiss these people.) Such notes may earn an idea fee, but you'll get none of the other credits that a freelancer banks on—bylines or clips or calls from the editor to write something else.

Your query letter must have an air of confidence about it. In a later section, we'll discuss how to tell the editor of your experience (or get around your lack of it), but even when you're outlining your idea, you must use language that says to the editor, "I can do this."

An essential element in this is knowing what you're proposing. Have you thought the article through? If you're going to offer a list of ten tips, do you know what the ten will be? If the editor asked, could you name all five of the great undiscovered ski resorts? I'll grant you that this doesn't leave a lot of room for research, but it's better for the beginning writer—whose reputation is largely a blank slate—to have done more than enough research before writing a query than to have not done enough.

Beyond being able to present a thorough picture of the article you're proposing, you must write confidently. Say "I will" instead of "I hope to." Say "This article will show your readers . . ." rather than "I think your readers will see . . ." And when previewing the sources you'll talk to for information, let the editor see you are presenting more than a wish list. "I've already contacted Clive Cussler, David Morrell and

Elmore Leonard about contributing to my article on plotting" inspires far more confidence in editors than "I'd like to contact several well-known authors for their thoughts." (Or, one of my personal favorites, "Can you supply the addresses of authors who might be willing to talk to me regarding this topic?")

Whatever tone you adopt for your letter, employ it consistently through your letter. Don't let your bright and breezy opening turn into a sodden morass in paragraph two; the editor will decide you can't maintain a consistent voice through a full article. I've said this before, and I'll say it again: Your query letter is the best indication an editor has of how you'll write if she assigns you an article. The letter you send must be your best work. And in this instance, I mean its high quality must be consistent from beginning to end.

Start with a piece of paper

I use this subhead knowing that at least a few readers will think the section that follows is written for the terminally dim. I promise you, however, that I will not be making a mountain out of a sheet of paper. I once saw a critique offered by a self-proclaimed (because no one else would say it) "literary critique service" that said the writer had typed on the wrong side of the paper. Such hairsplitting is ridiculous; for the most part, as with Stein's rose and Freud's cigar, a piece of paper is a piece of paper is a piece of paper. But there are a couple of common-sense rules regarding the paper on which you type your letter.

The paper should be white. You can stretch that to include letter-head that is off-white or even a light gray, but—please—no reds, yellows, greens, oranges, violets, limes, pinks or blues. Sometimes new writers pick a bright color with the idea that it'll make their letters stand out from the pack. It will, but not in the way the writer hoped. This is one area where you should follow the pack. Stick to good old-fashioned white.

The weight of the paper—that is, its thickness—is not a matter of particular concern. A nice 20-pound stationery-quality page is just fine, but so is the ream you swipe from the company photocopy machine. (Note to management: Not that *I* would ever do such a thing. But I understand others do such deplorable acts. Tsk, tsk.) Do not use erasable bond. It's crinkly, it feels funny, and it smears like crazy.

Feed your paper into a typewriter or a computer printer. No hand-written queries. And put type on that page using a new black ribbon. No exceptions.

Every other question regarding the mechanics of typing your letter can probably be answered by asking yourself, Which option is the most readable? Editors make their livings with their eyes; it's tough to read queries, manuscripts, galleys, page proofs and subpoenas without them. So we look favorably on writers who don't tax our most precious organs. Just to be sure, though, here's the official line on the most common questions:

- "Should I use a letter-quality computer printer or is dot matrix OK?" Use of the term "OK" suggests which is the more readable option. However, today's dot matrix printers produce type that is far clearer than the earliest nine-pin eye mashers. So the dot matrix prohibitions have pretty much fallen by the wayside. Still, laser and ink-jet printers produce a much finer look.
- "What size type should I use? Pica or elite?" A ten-point pica typeface is easy on the eyes without also having the appearance of a first-grade reader. You didn't ask this, but don't feel the need to change fonts and point sizes just because your word-processing program allows you to. And hold off on the italic and bold typefaces, too. If you must, it's acceptable to underline.
- "Where should I set the margins?" Aim for an inch to an inch and a half all around. Remember, no one will be laying a ruler against your letter. But less than an inch gives the page a cramped feel, more than an inch and a half seems too airy.
- "Are editors this picky about everything?" How do you think we got to be editors?

Dear . . . Who?

A query letter (or, worse, a complete manuscript) that is simply addressed to "The Editor" is received in a magazine's offices with all the respect you give a letter addressed to "Occupant." Such mail is consigned to the deepest recesses of the "slush pile," which is the ever-so-empathetic name the magazine industry has given to the stacks of unsolicited article submissions. So it is vital that you address your query letter to a specific editor at your target publication.

Finding this name is not terribly difficult. *Writer's Market* includes in most of its listings the name of the editor who reviews submissions. Generally, a magazine only provides *WM* with the name of the editor who reviews features. But, as I mentioned previously, you may stand a better chance of getting your first assignment from a magazine if you aim for one of its departments. Departments are often handled by someone other than the editor reviewing features. So where do you find *this* person's name?

The simplest way to get the name is to call the magazine's editorial offices. Yes, editors always tell freelancers that they hate phone calls from writers they don't know, but this is an exception. First, it should be one of the shortest phone calls you ever make. The complete transcript should go something like this. "Hello. Could you tell me the name of the editor who handles queries for the Writing Life department of your magazine? [The name is given.] Thank you." Click. Second, you don't need to even speak with an editor. When you call the magazine, ask the operator who answers the phone to connect you to the editorial department. Pose your question to whomever answers that phone. If that person initiates a more detailed discussion, fine. It's rare, but writers have been asked to pitch their ideas over the phone when they've called for a name. So you might want to be prepared.

What if you run into an obstinate sort who refuses to give you a name? After considering whether you still want to work with such difficult souls, you can probably find the name within the pages of the magazine. Your first stop is the masthead, which is a list of the magazine's staff. It's usually found in the first few pages of each issue. Your target editor may have a title incorporating the department name, such as Beauty Editor or Articles Editor—Departments. Also check the department itself. Many include an "edited by" credit near the department logo.

If none of these sources pans out, go back to the masthead. Pick out the editor most likely to review manuscripts, and address your letter to her. Your first choice would be the editor with the title Articles Editor. Not every magazine has an articles editor, however; my next choice would be the Managing Editor. My third choice would be the Associate (or Assistant) Editor. Although you might assume otherwise, the Editor would be my last choice; reviewing unsolicited submissions is nearly always the work of a junior editor. The exception to this would be a very small magazine with a two-person staff. In such cases, I'd address my letter to the editor.

If your target editor's name comes from any source other than a phone call to the magazine, I'd recommend calling the publication to verify it. As many as four months can pass between a magazine's preparation and its arrival in your mailbox, and turnover within the editing profession is legendary. A quick phone call costs practically nothing and can save your query from being routed from desk to desk to slush pile.

Once you learn who you're writing to, you can turn your attention to the letter itself. If you didn't realize it before, you should by now recognize that this isn't a letter to Grandma. The stakes are much higher here: Grandma loves you unconditionally; editors do not. You may never have revised a letter in your life, but your first queries will likely require multiple drafts until you've distilled the idea to a page or two and settled on a friendly, consistent tone.

Luckily, the best queries follow a three-part structure. I'll outline that structure, and show you multiple examples of successful queries, in the following three chapters.

CHAPTER FOUR

Opening Your Letter

You're faced with a stack of letters. The mail boy just dropped maybe a dozen on your desk, and that's in addition to yesterday's twenty. You know what each contains: an article idea from a freelancer. You've got that meeting with the art director in an hour, but with luck you can knock these out and still have time to grab a cola before she shows up.

As a freelance writer, that's the scenario you face each time one of your query letters lands on the desk of a magazine editor. As an editor, my immediate task is to work through this pile before it becomes a mountain. Sure, I'm looking for good article ideas, but experience teaches me that most days I won't find one. So I move through them as quickly as I can. I'm reading, but perhaps I'm also thinking of the upcoming meeting, or how I'm gonna come up with the money to repair my car, or even the poor state of spelling among freelancers today. Your immediate task is to stop my assembly line of open, scan, reject. And the only way you can accomplish that goal is to craft an opening that grabs my attention. Your letter's first paragraphs must figuratively stand up and yell, *"HEY! Look at Me!"*

Does this goal sound familiar to you? It's the same task every writer assigns to the first paragraphs of an article. There, too, the goal is to hook your readers, to grab them by the lapels and hang on until it's too late for them to turn back—that is, until they are emotionally involved in your story. The techniques for doing so are many, and, with some adjustment, these approaches can be adapted for use in a query letter.

The key difference between writing the lead of an article and the opening of a query letter concerns length. In a feature article, your lead can run on for a few hundred words. One of my favorite article leads opened an Eric Pooley *New York Magazine* article called "Dave's Kids." The lead is an extended anecdote that takes readers behind the scenes of a particularly zany *Late Night With David Letterman* show. It's a funny incident that loses none of its humor in the retelling. It's also an attention-grabbing lead. But Pooley's opening runs more than 300 words—more words than the query letter writer may use in a whole letter. For comparison's sake, I counted the words in one of my query letters; it totaled just 214 words.

The straightforward approach

Even though it may have hundreds of fewer words, the opening of your query letter must have all the impact of an article lead. Efficiency is critical; the fewer words you spend in setup means you'll have all the more words to describe your idea. The best leads are straightforward. You must attack your topic.

> In the last year or two, the Northwest has had a surfeit of meetings about declining salmon runs. While government, industry and environmental leaders have been arguing, high school students in the tiny town of Cathlamet near the mouth of the Columbia River have been rearing Chinook salmon fry.

Writer Sally-Jo Bowman's opening gave the editor of *Wildlife Conservation* some critical information in this straightforward opening. She set up the topic—salmon—and its relevance to *Wildlife Conservation*—"declining salmon runs." She also indicated that her approach to this topic was out of the ordinary; it's obvious from just this first paragraph that Bowman isn't proposing yet another article that centers on the "surfeit of meetings." In fact, her lead promises to take the magazine's readers as far from the corridors of power as it's possible to go: to a group of high school students.

The advantages of straightforward openings are clear. Because you launch into the topic immediately, even the dimmest editor will be right with you. There is little chance to lose her (unless the editor simply has no interest in your topic). But distilling the essence of your story idea into a short, neat paragraph is more allusive.

Begin by asking yourself what makes your story worthy of attention; often this will be what first attracted you to the idea. Then craft a paragraph that clearly communicates that this element is your hook, the angle you've taken that makes your idea different. You may remember from your high school composition classes that the "power position" of a sentence—the spot that hits readers most forcefully—is right before the period. That's true of paragraphs as well. In Bowman's example above, she held off mentioning the high schoolers (unusual players in a conservation story) until the last sentence of her lead—and the students' act of rearing salmon fry until the last words.

The "surprise" opening

Many writers look to pack more wallop into their openings by including a "surprise." The surprise could be: a clever turn of phrase, a startling statistic, an unexpected quote, a shocking situation. The intent is to shake the editor from her open-scan-reject routine and to get her to pay closer attention as she continues reading this particular letter.

> When my son came home from his friend's house and said to me, "Danny showed me his dad's gun," I nearly fainted dead away.
> —*Carol Silverman Saunders*

> Here's my darkest professional secret: G.P. Putnam's Sons could have offered me $10,000 less for *How to Fire Your Boss* and I'd have taken it. I was *that* elated to have a big international house publish my first book. Now nine books later, I'm less starry-eyed. My literary career has all the profit oriented aspects of my other business interests.
> —*Christopher R. Malburg*

> Getting smacked in the head with an egg may not sound like much fun, but in San Antonio, Texas, it is a long-standing tradi-

tion believed to bring good luck. Of course, the eggs are hollow and filled with confetti—all 100,000 of them!
　　—Carla Joinson

All three of these queries begin with a bang calculated to make an editor sit up and take notice. Yet the magnitude of these bangs vary. Only Carol Silverman Saunders's statement could be considered earth-shaking. Sent to *Parents* magazine, her letter's opening immediately addresses a fear very much on the minds of today's mothers (and, therefore, of editors speaking to those mothers). Also working in Saunders's favor is the way this paragraph establishes her experience with the topic and, thus, the personal expertise she will bring in writing this article on gun safety awareness.

Malburg's lead also quickly sets up his credentials: He's a successful book writer who once let emotions get in the way of sound business practices. This information carries me into the second paragraph where Malburg gives a capsule description of the article he wants to write for *Writer's Digest*.

Joinson's query was pitched to the editors of *Spark!*, a now-defunct magazine specializing in art projects for children. There's a lot of child-like glee in her first sentence, a quality that shows Joinson's ability to identify with (and, by extension, write for) the audience. And, as *Spark!* editor Beth Struck said, "How could an editor not be curious enough to read beyond 'Getting smacked in the head with an egg . . .'?"

There is a dark side to relying on surprising statements: What may be surprising to you may not raise an eyebrow of someone who routinely watches that particular field. The editor of one women's magazine told me, "I'm a tough audience because I have to be well read" to recognize new trends that will be of interest to readers. "To tell me a surprising statistic that I don't know takes some research," she said. Overplaying a surprise statistic or new research not only fails to capture an editor's attention, but also has the unfortunate effect of branding you as a neophyte on the topic.

You must also be wary of overacting. If Malburg's "darkest professional secret" had been something as common as, say, that he sold his first book without an agent, my chuckle would have been reduced to a groan. There's humor in the idea of a writer willing to take less money (not to mention a publisher paying more than it had to), enough humor to draw me into the rest of the letter with my antennae alert. The opening's mission accomplished, Malburg's second sentence is down to business, in the manner of a straightforward opening. He doesn't depend on the joke to do anything more than open the door.

While the bang of a surprising statement can jolt the inattentive editor, don't get burned in a misdirected blast. If you haven't found something surprising in your research so far and a relevant twist of phrase escapes you, then you're better off crafting a straightforward approach. Trust me: Trying too hard for something clever is always worse than a thoughtful, well-phrased opening.

Leading with a question

I find dangers, too, in posing a question in your first sentence. These leads try to elicit a response from the editor: "Have you ever wondered why the swallows return to Capistrano?" might be an example. But in asking such a question, my fear as a writer is that the editor will respond with a question of her own, something along the lines of "Who cares?"

Certainly not the response I'm looking for.

That doesn't mean I've never made an assignment from such a letter or that some of my best friends aren't questions. If you're going to ask an editor a question, you must carefully consider what you'll be asking. The editor who might consider a story on either Capistrano or the birds therein has likely already read a couple dozen Capistrano stories in her tenure. Putting such a—to her mind—mundane question as your opening, tells the editor you have nothing new to add to this old discussion.

Much better is the question that challenges the editor. Larry Hartsfield began his letter to *Delta Air Lines Sky Magazine* with this question:

> What could *Family Feud* and *Family Ties*, *The Cosby Show* and *thirtysomething* possibly have in common, other than being watched and enjoyed by millions of Americans?

Hartsfield's question might be called a riddle—a sophisticated cousin of "What's white and black and red all over?" It challenges the editor to see a connection between two or more items that otherwise seem to have nothing in common. (In Hartsfield's case, he removes the one obvious commonality—the TV shows' success—from the playing field.) The goal is to capture the editor's attention by piquing her curiosity. Hartsfield's riddle works for me because those four television programs were pretty diverse offerings. I want to know what ties them together.

As with any riddle, the success of your opening will be determined by the question's answer—its "punch line." And that answer must come quickly; you've posed the challenge, and the editor will expect you to solve the puzzle before anything else happens. And if you don't provide the answer, my mind will keep looking for a solution, and I won't be paying close attention to any other words you write. Hartsfield knows this, and provides the answer in the very next sentence:

> These and practically every other program from TV's beginning to the present are now being subjected more and more to the straining, stretching, poking and prodding of semioticians, structuralists, exegetes and deconstructionists as they "mine" the daily TV schedule for insights into the values, beliefs and behaviors of Americans.

Wisely, Hartsfield leads off his second paragraph with a second question—"Who are these semioticians and deconstructors?"—and the more important answer. Anytime you use terminology that might be unfamiliar to the editor (and her readers), furnish a definition quickly. Editors left confused by a query are not editors likely to offer an assignment.

It was Carol-Lynn Marrazzo's question that captured our interest at *Writer's Digest*:

> Would you be interested in a piece that debunks the "show, don't tell" principle of fiction writing?"

Any fiction writer who's been writing more than a month will tell you that "show, don't tell" is the most intoned of writing's holy commandments. It is the mantra of writing instructors everywhere and, not coincidentally, the topic of numerous articles in *WD*. Since her challenge of that advice is what makes Marrazzo's article unique, she wisely puts that punch in the first sentence. The question is a sure-bet come-on; as an editor, I could no more turn away from this opening than I could if someone were to ask me, "Would you like to make a million dollars?"

For the record, it is only the originality of Marrazzo's topic that lets her get away with the otherwise unoriginal phrase, "Would you be interested in a piece . . ." This chestnut shows up far too often in the slush pile and carries all the appeal of a stink bomb. Why? First, its passive construction generates no energy that might transfer to whatever topic follows (remember, I said it was Marrazzo's topic that made the line tempting). Second, it's the straight line that makes the editor's rebuttal easy: "No thanks, already got one." And last, it's redundant. The whole purpose of a query letter is to ask, "Would you be interested in a piece on . . ." As Marrazzo's letter proves, there are times when posing a question can be the appropriate lead. Just make sure you're asking a question whose answer will lead into the rest of your letter.

Opening with your article's lead

The goal of opening a query letter and opening an article are so similar that one of the most frequently repeated pieces of advice regarding queries is to simply pick up your article's opening and use it in your query letter as well. And that can work . . . up to a point. But I have problems with that advice. First, it assumes you've written the article before you've written the query. But that's thinking backward: You write the query to determine if there's interest in the idea and, if there is, to what audience the article should be slanted. So you shouldn't have a prewritten opening laying about waiting to be slipped into your query. My second problem with the advice is an article opening is written to lead into the rest of the article. A query letter's opening must direct the editor into a discussion of your idea and how you'll pursue that idea in your article. Too often, the only sentence the letter writer can find to follow a transplanted article lead is "That's how I'll open my article." I've seen it so much that it's become a cliché—tired and lifeless. And if the lead succeeded in yelling *"HEY!,"* that follow-up line whispers "Uh, never mind."

This is not to say that transplanting doesn't occur. Here's the first paragraph of a query letter I wrote to *Modern Bride* magazine:

Shortly before the wedding day, my soon-to-be mother-in-law

fixed me with a stare from across the dinner table. "No mother-in-law jokes. OK?" Our good rapport over the seven years since has only partially been due to my honoring her request. And the few major disagreements have come when I forgot "The Key to Getting 'In' With Your In-Laws."

I'll reveal that key in . . .

Compare that paragraph to this one, which is the opening of the article that resulted from the query:

Shortly before my wedding day, my mother-in-law-to-be fixed me with a hard stare from across the dining room table. "No mother-in-law jokes. OK?"

Our pleasant—even loving—relationship since then is based only partially on my remembering that promise (and that stare). In larger measure, I've stayed "in" with my in-laws because I realize that my wife's parents remain just that—parents—and that they continue to have a commitment to their daughter that is, in its way, as strong as our wedding vows.

This was a case when the evocative anecdote was a natural opening for both query and article. For the article, I moved from the incident into a preview of the overall philosophy at work in this piece: In-laws remain your spouse's parents, and you must learn to live with that fact. The query letter required a different segue, from anecdote to a statement of the letter's purpose: to propose an article of interest to *Modern Bride*'s readers.

(We'll examine the rest of that letter in later chapters. Try not to look ahead.)

Shine the spotlight on you

I once heard an editor say that a query letter had to tell him two things: Why now and why you? In most cases, you'll address these issues farther into your letter (as I'll explain in the next two chapters). But for some articles, the answer to "Why you?" will be your central selling point. For whatever reason, only *you* can do this story—and the opening of your letter is the best place to make sure the editor understands this.

As the editor of *Ladies' Home Journal*'s "A Woman Today" column—our true-life personal-experience feature—I've read hundreds upon hundreds of unsolicited manuscripts by both novices and seasoned writers. I've seen poignant accounts of children recovering from cancer; I've cheered women finding the courage to escape abusive marriages; I've been heartened by the tales of heroes of every sort.

I've also read more than my share of labored humor essays on the ordeal of doing the laundry, twenty-page musings inspired by the sight of the first crocus of the season, and "Grandma Remembers Christmas on the Farm."

It is intriguing to note that nowhere in these two paragraphs does the writer Shana Aborn, mention the article she's pitching. Her subject is herself—in particular her experience in reading and editing a specific type of magazine article. Not surprisingly, how to write this type of article is the topic of the article Aborn wanted to write. And because of how she establishes herself in the opening, I already recognize Aborn as an authority on the topic when she begins to discuss her plan for the article.

The effect would not have been the same if Aborn had let her opening drift away from her experiences in reading personal experience articles. If she'd also mentioned profiles and how-to features or talked about jobs she'd held before coming to *LHJ*, my attention would not have been focused on her true-life drama expertise when she began to outline her proposed article.

This is a bit like being a ringmaster at a three-ring circus. At any one point in time, stagehands may be assembling the tiger cages or performers may be collecting their props following their acts, but most audience members will never notice them. The ringmaster's patter and the spotlight's beam are directing the audience's attention to the ring where a new act is underway. The stagehands' tasks may be intriguing, but if the ringmaster allows our eyes to wander over there, we'll miss the real entertainment—the stuff we'll enjoy enough to make us want to come back next year.

A personal opening can vary in how much attention you focus on yourself and how much on your relationship to the topic you're proposing. Let's look at two more excerpts to see the extremes.

I'd already sold the editor of *Modern Bride* the in-laws relationship article when I wrote this query. Because we'd recently spoken on the phone regarding a contractual matter, I took a couple lines to thank her for her time and her acceptance of the previous piece. Then I got down to new business:

> I have an idea that I think will also be of service to your readers. Certainly it would have been of benefit to my wife and I shortly after we were married. My wife's a nurse, and her career demanded that she return to school for a master's degree. In the two years that she split time between the hospital, campus and our house, we made a lot of adjustments and had to establish priorities for what would get done and what we'd put off until after graduation.
>
> My brother and his wife dealt with many of the same concerns. They met and married while Brian was still a student; Patti was establishing a career. And we see a half dozen friends working through the process as one or the other returns to campus.

My expertise with this topic was that I had lived it—that I was intimately acquainted with the adjustments and priority-setting that are required during such a period in a marriage. I also wanted to convince *Modern Bride*'s editor that my wife and I weren't the only couple experiencing this particular stress on our marriage; we were, in fact, part of a trend. This experience, I hoped to say, was something at least a portion of her readers would soon face. So I enlarged the spotlight to show my brother and his wife and a glimpse of the other people just beyond the beam I was shining on the subject. My aim was to show that I was in position to bring personal experience and personal contacts together in a way another writer might not. A straightforward lead, stripped of my experience and addressing only the topic of marital survival when your spouse goes back to school, would not have achieved that effect.

In a query to *Writer's Digest*, Mubarak S. Dahir spends three paragraphs recounting his personal path to freelancing success. Just try to guess the focus of the article he eventually pitches.

Just four years ago, I was taking lighting measurements in a basement laboratory at Penn State University, dreading finishing my master's degree and taking a nine-to-five job as an architectural engineer. I had never written a magazine story, much less sold one. I didn't even know what a query letter was.

Today, I am the Philadelphia stringer for *Time* magazine, a columnist for the *Philadelphia Daily News*, an editor at the *Philadelphia City Paper*, and have written for such national publications as *Omni, Modern Maturity, Men's Fitness* and American Airlines' magazine.

So was there this well of raw talent I just never knew existed until it one day bubbled through? While that explanation is tempting, it isn't accurate. The truth is, I took a course on how to write—and, perhaps more importantly, how to sell—magazine articles. Soon after, I left graduate school and became a freelance writer.

Dahir's topic was an introduction to writing and selling magazine articles. His hook was a promise to show *WD*'s readers how to "do the same thing" he'd done. But before Dahir could make that promise, he had to show me what he'd done. His is a classic rags-to-riches story (or, considering a freelancer's profit potential, a rags-to-slightly-better-rags story), so Dahir could allow the query's opening to linger solely on himself. He even takes the time to discount one possible explanation for his success—the "well of raw talent" theory—which, if believed by the editor reading the letter, would call into question whether Dahir could guide *WD*'s readers down the same path. He not only told me his story, but also set me up to believe he could offer lessons to others.

One last trick

A few paragraphs back I discussed the second query I sent to *Modern Bride*. I mentioned that before I launched into the query itself, I took a couple lines to thank the editor for a recent phone call and for buying the first article, which I mentioned by name. I was being sincere in my expression of gratitude, but those first couple of lines also worked to my advantage. Even if the editor hadn't recognized my name on the letterhead, that referral to the phone call and previous article would have reminded her that we had already worked together—that she had previously judged one of my ideas to be useful to her audience.

And there are worse associations people could make.

Obviously, this tactic is best applied when you're querying an editor with whom you've already worked. But you can adapt it to first letters—"cold calls," as they're called by salespeople. Writer Sally-Jo Bowman, whom I quoted earlier in this chapter, had an idea for *Audubon* magazine, a market she had not previously appeared in. Here's how she opened her letter to the magazine's editor:

> My colleague Mark Hoy suggested you would be the right person to query on "Trouble in Paradise."

Bowman's lead establishes an immediate beachhead with the *Audubon* editor for three reasons: First, she connects herself to someone the editor knows. This says, in effect, "He's worked for you and thinks I'm someone you could work with, too." (This is a bit risky, of course; if the editor doesn't like the person you name, those feelings will likely be transferred to you as well.) Second, Bowman indicates that she's done enough research on *Audubon* to seek out advice from a colleague whose work has appeared there. And, third, Bowman wastes no time moving into her article idea. She could have just as easily written "to query with my idea for an article." But by naming the article, she lets it plant a couple questions in the editor's mind: What trouble? Which paradise? The title becomes a hook to keep the editor reading.

As a new writer, whether you're a beginner overall or simply new to a particular market, you need to use whatever tactics you can find to make an impression on the editor who opens your letter. Whatever connection you can make with an editor is better than making a completely cold call. I speak frequently at writers' conferences and often receive queries from people who have met me there. I don't bite on them all, of course, but I generally respond to them myself, rather than passing them on to the editorial assistant who handles the "faceless" slush. Especially if the writer has said nice things about my talk. Or reminds me that he bought me a drink. Commenting nicely on something the editor wrote in the magazine is a similar approach. Just be sure your flattery is genuine and short; remember, the reason you're writing is to propose an article.

Which is my final point regarding the personal approach: This sort of lead-in is only a prelude to your real opening. A referral or other association may catch the editor's eye, but you must still hook the editor's interest in your idea. The only way to do that is with a dynamic and captivating first paragraph.

Which opening is best for you

I have one writing book in my library that lists fourteen types of leads that might kick off an article. There are anecdotal leads and single example leads and "you" leads and question leads and three variations of surprising leads (contrast, statement and quote, in case you were wondering). I figure that list is darn near exhaustive—maybe even a bit stretched since a few of the boundary lines between types are pretty thin.

As a writer, I don't like to dwell on such lists because they point out just how many choices I have when writing. And there are more than fourteen choices. Let's say that I decide I want to open an article with a surprising quote. I still must decide which one of all the quotes I've collected for this article is the most surprising quote.

That's not how it works, of course. I sit down to write my article and see in my notes that I have this pretty surprising quote and this poignant anecdote and this on-the-button case history and this fairly intriguing question. Decisions, decisions.

The writer of query letters faces the same sort of dilemma. What to open with?

If the gods are smiling on you, it's a no-brainer. One thought has lodged in that section of the brain devoted to prewriting, and it has defended itself against all challengers. A bonus: You like this intransigent opening. My advice is go with it. Accept the manna from heaven and write the letter. Then go sacrifice a goat in thanksgiving.

Unfortunately (unless you happen to be a goat,) such visitations are rare. More often, you must work for your opening.

Sit down with a few sheets of paper and a pencil. Tell the little editor that sits on your shoulder to take a break—the last thing you need right now is a hypercritical voice shooting down ideas before they're even fully formed. The little editor will have its chance later, after you've drafted the letter. Now is anything-goes time.

At the top of the page, write down your topic and your specific approach to the topic—your article's hook. Sum up the work you hope to write in one sentence. (This should all sound familiar; if not, go back to chapter three.) If somewhere along the way you've concocted a working title for the article, jot that down, too.

Further prime your creative pump by listing the essential characteristics of your target audience. "Men, age 30-45, upper-middle class and beyond, interested in being healthier" might be your notation for an idea you're sending to *Men's Health*. Then get more specific; exactly who in that audience will be drawn to your idea? "Guys who believe their mothers-in-law hate them, yet don't understand why" might be the readers of a piece on how to declare a truce with your in-laws.

Now ask yourself what is the most intriguing aspect—intriguing to you—that you've uncovered in developing this idea. This might be something out of your personal experience with the topic, or something you uncovered in your initial research, or an area you want to explore further. Whatever it is, write it down. Now ask what is likely to be the most intriguing aspect to the editor of your target market. Oh, come on! You've read a half dozen issues at least. You know the editor's work, how the magazine approaches topics, what its sensibilities are; all of this reflects on the editor's interests. Your market research gives you the background to make this judgment. Finally, ask yourself what is likely to be the most intriguing aspect to your target reader.

In the happy event that all three aspects concern the same bit of information, you've probably found the basis for your lead. If they don't, look for a common thread running through all three. Is it someone's story (even your own)? Is it some failure of common wisdom? Is it new information? Whatever it is, isolate that thread and begin to play with it.

What you're doing here is sometimes called "freewriting." The idea is to put words on paper as quickly as possible, without stopping to critique or even consider what you wrote. In this instance, you want to concentrate on an opening line—or two or three, but no more than a paragraph. Sketch out straightforward statements and surprises and questions and anecdotes and whatever else comes to mind, no matter how much of a stretch it may seem. Do this for at least ten or fifteen minutes—longer if the words keep coming. Then lay down your pencil, walk away, and do something else for a while.

When you come back, you may find a new possibility lurking near the tip of your brain. Write it down before you review your earlier efforts, lest it dart back into the dark recesses of your brain. Then review your complete list. Circle those lines that seem to set off a little charge when you read them over, those lines that tickle your fancy however lightly. Pull those out for further consideration. You may need to work them over a bit—revising words here and there, restructuring the presentation, maybe recasting the tone—but this is where you'll find the basis for an opening that will capture your editor's attention and lead her into the midsection of your query.

First things last

Of all the questions I get asked about query letters, one of the most frequent concerns the letter's salutation. Most people get the "Dear" part, but the questions arise over the editor's name. (We've already covered the importance of addressing the letter to a specific editor.)

The only truly wrong answer to this question is to address the editor by her first name (or worse, a diminutive of her first name). It is acceptable to use either the editor's first and last name ("Dear Thomas Clark:") or the appropriate courtesy title, *Mr.*, *Ms.*, *Miss* or *Mrs.*, and last name. The latter, of course, opens up the *Miss-Mrs.-Ms.* debate. While *Ms.* is a standard usage these days, and perhaps even the safest bet, I usually avoid the whole briar patch and address my letter using the editor's first and last names.

CHAPTER FIVE

The Heart of the Query

We've seen that the first paragraph or two of your query letter are designed to grab the editor's attention. The middle section of your letter is where you capitalize on that prize: The goal here is to *sell* your idea. In these paragraphs, you must convince the editor that the story you're proposing is complete, compatible with the magazine's slant, and of value to the readers.

This is also where your writing skills will be examined and judged. Editors are as concerned with the writing in a query letter as they are with the idea being discussed. If the editor is unable to follow this synopsis of your idea, she's not likely to give you the chance to do better in a full-length article.

The sell copy

I think the middle paragraphs of a query letter have much in common with direct mail letters. You probably know these letters as "junk mail"—a term, by the way, guaranteed to drive any direct marketer out of the room in a fury. (Remember that tip; it can be very handy at parties.) A direct mail letter, as promotion department folks prefer to call junk mail, has just one goal: to sell you something. Might be a credit card, a magazine subscription, some variety of overpriced insurance, lawn care services, the plight of some worthy charity, or a hundred other products; whatever it is, it requires you to write a check.

Because most of us avoid writing checks whenever possible, direct marketers must employ all the powers of persuasion they possess. They must make you believe that you need this credit card, magazine subscription, insurance or whatever to find true happiness on this little rock in space.

This is not unlike the writer's strategy of convincing an editor that her magazine will be incomplete without the article the writer is proposing.

Here, for instance, is part of a letter that asked me to renew my child's subscription to *Zillions*, a magazine for children published by *Consumer Reports*. See the persuasion at work:

> Manufacturers will spend a record $450 million this year trying to reach your child through TV advertising alone . . . and the average child will watch enough TV to soak up more than 520 commercials a week.
>
> Advertising to your child might not be fair, truthful or even legal, but it is a fact of life. That's why I hope you and your child will come back to *Zillions*.
>
> Providing your children with *Zillions* is one of the best ways to help them sort through overblown claims, misleading ads and hyped-up products.
>
> *Zillions* teaches your children how to choose. How to resist the pressures that encourage them to spend indiscriminately. And how to have a healthy skepticism toward advertising.

The "you" statements are even more pointed in this letter from the American Civil Liberties Union, seeking a membership renewal:

> Losing you—or any other member—hurts the ACLU and weakens our ability to defend liberties. What's more, it's a weakening that could affect you <u>very directly</u>.
>
> You see, when you write the check that renews your commitment to defending liberties, you're making an impact very close to home. <u>Because more than half your contribution will go to support the work of the ACLU office in your home state</u>.

In *The Elements of Business Writing* (Collier Books), authors Gary Blake and Robert W. Bly point out that "the major difference between writing to inform and writing to persuade is one of intent." Both styles of writing, they continue, value clarity, precision and organization. But, "most business writing goes one step beyond the mere transmission of information and seeks . . . to motivate the reader to take some specific action."

Blake and Bly touch on a key point that most freelancers forget when they sit down to write a query letter. Because the freelancer is proposing a magazine article, the writer naturally believes his forte is informational writing. Indeed, the editor must come to share this belief before she'll make an assignment. But for the writer to encourage this realization in the editor's mind, the writer must write a persuasive letter. As Blake and Bly indicate, this is a different sort of animal. Writing to inform and writing to persuade share many characteristics, of course, but the letter that simply proposes an article may not be good enough. Your letters must also persuade an editor to ask you to write the article.

Blake and Bly name eight "principles of persuasion." I list them all below, although a couple are only marginally useful when writing the query letter. Obviously, there's more to be said on some of these points, and you'll hear echoes of Blake and Bly's points as we move through this chapter.

- "Gain your reader's attention in an appropriate manner." You'll recognize this from the discussion on openings in the previous chapter.
- "Awaken a need for an idea before presenting the idea." Take it as a given that the editor knows she needs articles for her magazine. But the editor may not know of the situation your proposed article will address or may not fully understand how that situation could impact the magazine's readers.
- "Stress benefits, not features." As you plan your article and write your query letter, you must always be thinking of how the information will benefit the magazine's readers. "Why will my readers care?" is a legitimate question, and every editor will ask it of every query. So yours better hold the answer.

- "Use facts, opinions and statistics to prove your case." Two good rules of thumb: An expert's opinions are better than yours, and facts and statistics are better than opinions.

- "Don't get bogged down in unnecessary details or arguments." Especially in these letters, concision matters.

- "Tell the reader what to do next." This is one of the marginal principles for query letter writers. The editor knows what you want her to do next; after all, there's only one reason for you to send a query letter. Still, in the next chapter we'll look at how some writers say this without insulting either their own or the editor's intelligence.

- "Before making a request, give the reader a reason to respond." Another marginal one, since it often results in such hackneyed lines as, "I hope you'll decide to share this groundbreaking new research with your readers." (Which I guess is better than "Please allow me to write this article for you so you'll have something to put in the next issue"!)

- "Do not assume the reader has been persuaded by your argument." Blake and Bly's point is to avoid such phrases as "I'm sure you agree . . ." and "As you know . . ." because the reader may not agree or know, and your assumption to the contrary will simply bring out the reader's disagreement. It's a minor point for query writers, but a good one. Any language that antagonizes the editor is bad language for a query.

Of course, a query letter is not synonymous with a letter hawking financial services or a vacation home in the swamps of Florida. If nothing else, the query is more subtle—both in its language and in its presentation. There's no need for underlining key phrases or typing impact words in all capital letters. And don't even think of loading up the red ribbon on your printer.

But as writers, we can learn a trick or two from those who are able to persuade consumers (like me) to renew those subscriptions and memberships. Your safest financial strategy may be to deliver most junk—er, direct—mail directly from the mailbox to the garbage can. But before you make your pitch, spend a few minutes studying theirs. Note how they attempt to persuade you, and consider how you might adapt these strategies in your own letters of persuasion.

Revealing your plan

We've said the goal of a query letter's middle section is to sell the story idea to the editor. To accomplish that task, you must tell the editor what sort of finished article you intend to write. You must explain your topic and your hook and show how you'll present your information. You must reveal your plan for the manuscript. (This means, of course, that you must *have* a plan for the manuscript. If your article idea isn't developed enough to provide the editor with the kinds of information that we'll discuss below, you need to do some more preliminary work. It's better to have on hand more information than you can put in your query than to have your idea rejected because you didn't provide enough support.)

This is where the query letter's critical balancing act comes in. To *completely* reveal your plan would be to tell the editor everything you plan to write in the article. This is called, of course, writing the article. And the query letter's purpose is to avoid writing a full-blown article until an editor has expressed an interest in seeing it. But if you reveal too little of your plan, the editor won't be intrigued enough to make the assignment. So how much must you tell?

The glib answer is, "As much as necessary, and not one sentence more." Before you throw up your hands in disgust, read that response again. It's a better guide than it initially appears to be.

Every piece of writing can be reduced to one sentence. Be it a novel, nonfiction book, article, short story, poem, script or whatever, you can capture its essence in just a few words. In *The Hunt for Red October*, for example, "a nearly silent Soviet nuclear submarine attempts to defect to the United States." Does that sentence capture the action, adventure and drama of Tom Clancy's book? Of course not, but the sentence isn't meant to replace the book. It only encapsulates the plot of the book. The book you're holding could be summed up this way, "Advice on how to write query letters that will win article assignments from editors." That sentence doesn't offer any of the advice, but it does tell you the advice is in the book.

Figuring out the sentence that describes your article is an excellent starting point for writing the middle portion of your query letter. Craft it carefully, however; make sure it captures the essence of your article. Notice that the line I used to describe this book doesn't neglect the benefit that I hope you, the reader, will receive for your time and money. That benefit is what I hope distinguishes this book from other letter-writing books, so I wanted that benefit reflected in the summation sentence. Benefit to the reader is a key element that editors look for in article proposals, and the best query letters come from writers who emphasize that element—from the very first sentence.

You may or may not actually use this summation sentence in your query letter. But it will be the backbone that supports the rest of your "sell copy"; every other sentence will radiate from it.

Those additional sentences will simply build on the theme sounded by that summation sentence, adding broad strokes to the canvas until the editor can picture the manuscript you're proposing. How many sentences you need is determined by a combination of factors: the complexity of your topic, how you've chosen to tell the story, your personal writing style, the type of market you're writing for, even your familiarity with the editor. There will be times when you feel you must present a longer letter; other times you'll sense a need to be even briefer than usual. Overall, though, I think you'll find after you write a few of these paragraphs that it doesn't take a great number of sentences to give an editor a solid overview of your idea.

In the last chapter, I gave you the opening of a query letter I wrote to *Modern Bride* proposing an article on getting along with your in-laws. Here's the sell copy I crafted for that letter (for continuity's sake, I'm picking up the last line of the first paragraph):

> And the few major disagreements have come when I forgot "The Key to Getting 'In' With Your In-Laws."
>
> I'll reveal that key in a 1,500-word article that will help your readers avoid run-ins with their new in-laws. It's a simple strategy of remembering that these people are—after all—parents and of responding to potential conflicts accordingly. I'll use examples from my own marriage and from others' to show the strategy in action—and even how it can be used to combat the often bitter husband-wife clashes that center on each other's parents.

Not very long, is it? Just eighty words in that paragraph. But each sentence builds on the previous one, and each adds to the editor's understanding of what my completed manuscript would include. This article's hook is the notion that there's a "key" to unlocking the in-law dilemma. I refer to that key in both the title and in the next paragraph's initial sentence. I then define the key in the second sentence and promise to show readers how to use it. Finally, the third sentence explains what proof I'll offer to show readers that this key works in real life. And both the first and last sentences of this paragraph speak of a direct benefit to the reader ("help your readers avoid run-ins with their new in-laws" and "how it can be used to combat the often bitter husband-wife clashes").

Not every query letter will be this short; in fact, this may be about as brief a query letter as you're ever likely to send. Later on we'll look at letters that describe more complex topics, which require more sentences to provide the thorough overview an editor looks for. And sometimes your topic will require you to offer the editor more background information. (In my case, the need to familiarize *Modern Bride*'s editor with the topic was nil. Anyone who's been married knows about in-laws.) But, in general, writers should force themselves to think short—or at least short*er*. My experience is that writers want to spill more words in a query letter than are really necessary. Sometimes far more. Not too long ago, for example, I received a query letter from an author who wanted to write about how to research a novel. His letter went on for *four pages*. In the course of proposing the story, he told me about all (at least it seemed like all) his adventures in discovering the story behind some real-life incident that played a role in his novel. Needless to say, most of the letter was unnecessary. And, as you've also certainly figured out, the writer did not get the assignment.

Necessity sets the standard for what you tell an editor in a query letter. After reading my letter above, you undoubtedly still have questions about what my in-laws article will say. In my query, I don't go into any sort of depth to define this "key" (in fact, I devoted only about a dozen words to summarizing it). I don't give specifics about the tips I'll offer. And I don't preview any of the marital episodes that I promise to recount in the article. I don't because none of that was necessary to propose the article. Remember, editors don't want to read the article; they just want to come away from the letter believing that you have a solid idea of *how* to write it and that you *can* write it.

Drawing an outline

To turn skeptical editors into believers who trust your ability, you must show them your plan. An editor needs to believe that you've hit upon a topic and slant that are right for her magazine and that you've figured out how you'll present this package to readers.

Editors treat article assignments in the same manner civilians (that is, noneditors) handle the various proposals that arise in everyday life. Let's say, for example, that your spouse comes to you and announces that next summer your family will visit the Grand Canyon. (Note to readers in Arizona, New Mexico, Colorado and parts of California: If you fail to appreciate the magnitude of such a trip, substitute the words *Washington, D.C.* for *Grand Canyon.*)

"Whoa," you say, "How can we . . ."

"I know just what you're going to say," your spouse replies, "but I've got a plan: We can borrow the Smiths' camper trailer and tow it behind our van. If we start brown bagging our lunches and banking what we save, plus set aside the raises we each got last month, we should be able to swing the cost. I'm figuring we'll need about $150 a day. Yeah, it's a long drive, but if we can go out along a southern route and come back via the Midwest, we can see a whole lot of the country. I'm figuring we'll need to spend maybe six days on the road. That gives us four or five days at the canyon and a day to kill along the way."

"Well, OK," you say. "This just might work out."

Yes, there are details yet to be discussed and determined. But your spouse hasn't asked you to start packing, either. What you've got is a sense for the breadth of the operation and an appreciation that this is more than a spur-of-the-moment idea. Energy has been expended, the idea has been studied, and an outline for turning this wish into reality has been drafted. Unless you have no desire to stand on the South Rim and contemplate the insignificance of man in relation to nature, then you've got enough information to give your go-ahead for more research, detailed planning and, finally, execution.

Which is all every query-writing freelancer wants from an editor: a go-ahead to do more work.

Unfortunately, unsuccessful queries often fail to provide a sense of breadth or suggest that this is more than a spur-of-the-moment idea.

(A clarification at this point: From now on, when I talk of "unsuccessful queries," the reference will be to queries that propose a topic appropriate to the magazine, yet aren't judged worthy of assignment. As I've said elsewhere, the vast majority of the queries in the slush pile get rejected because the writer has failed to understand the needs of the magazine.)

There are many variations on this theme, but generally I reject queries for one of two reasons: Either the writer fails to tell me what slant he will bring to the topic, or the writer doesn't sufficiently outline how he'll execute his plan.

The first problem is a special bane to travel editors. They tell *Writer's Digest* that their most common rejected query letter can be summed up this way: "I recently returned from [or I am about to visit] fill-in-the-blank, and would like to write about this fascinating destination for your readers. Would you be interested in this article?" To rip off the hamburger ad, "Where's the hook?" This letter offers no clues as to what the writer will tell readers about the destination, what special nooks and crannies of the place will be highlighted, what theme will run through the article, what information the readers will take away. As I heard one travel editor put it at a writers' conference: "San Francisco is a destination, not an article idea." Your query must tell the editor what part of the subject you will write about—whether your subject is San Francisco or anything else.

From there you must explain how you will cover that part of the topic you've hung on your hook. If nothing else, you must show the editor that this hook is valid, that you've found enough to say to fill up an article. This is a basic expectation, however; most editors will want you to go further. They will want you to convince them that your article will be interesting and beneficial to readers. You do this by outlining the content of the article you're proposing.

Don't be scared off by the word *outlining*. You are no longer in high school; when you threw off your graduation robe, you also cast off the need for Roman numerals and letters and the requirement that every *A* must have its *B*. Instead, editors are looking for an explanation of how you'll mine the territory you've staked out for yourself. Here's a short example from JoAnn Greco, who convinced me to assign an article with this sell copy:

For *Writer's Digest* readers, I'd like to present "Trade Off: Writing for an Often-Neglected Market," a complete guide to the opportunities in trade magazines. I'll talk with editors to learn what they're looking for and writers to discuss how they entered the market. I'll also present my overview of the advantages (and disadvantages) of writing for trades, including

- clearly defined sense of who your audience is
- regular work with a particular publication once you break in
- light editing, quick payment
- total immersion in the mundane aspects of your industry
- often shaky line between advertising and editorial
- low prestige

Greco's one-line summation of her idea is right in the first sentence: "a complete guide to the opportunities in trade magazines." From there she elaborates on what will make up this "complete guide"; I know my readers will learn what editors want, they'll learn how other writers have broken in, and they'll learn at least six advantages and disadvantages to working in this field. The only area of interest missing from Greco's query is one more bit of how-to: an explanation of the specific writing techniques most often used by trade magazine freelancers. But the quality of her letter convinced me that Greco could deliver this additional element (which I asked for in my assignment letter).

One technique Greco uses in her sell copy is to list a variety of points she'll make in her article. Many writers would have left it at, "I'll present my overview of the advantages (and disadvantages) of writing for trades," period. But I think a list brings authority to a query. It sets the proposal in concrete. With this list in front of me, I don't have to wonder what the advantages and disadvantages are. I don't even have to wonder if *Greco* has decided what those advantages and disadvantages are. I know what Greco will tell my readers on this critical point because she listed the pros and cons up front.

Notice, too, what Greco *didn't* list. I have no details on the editors' needs or the writers' experiences—either of which she could have related in a list. Of the three components comprising her "complete guide," Greco elaborated only on the one that would mean the most to *WD*'s audience of freelancers.

Filling in your outline

Deciding what components of your article's outline you need to elaborate on can be tricky. In this query, freelancer Donald Ray Patterson unleashes a slew of examples to elaborate on his main topic: using your home computer as a gardening tool. But these elaborations operate only as examples to show the wide-ranging applications he'll discuss in the article.

Computerize your garden? Doesn't sound exciting, but in these days of the home computer revolution, hundreds of household tasks are becoming automated through the innovative application of these personal thinking machines.

So why not your garden? Just think of the time-savers you can generate with your home PC. You can draw your garden layout with a simple graphics program and update it to meet each phase of the growing season. You can use it to plan crop rotation and save yourself the trouble of marking your rows by putting planting information on your computer printout. Your home computer can also remember, plan and evaluate many of your tedious gardening maintenance chores. Use it to remind you of planting and anticipated maturity dates, when to apply what amount of fertilizer, when and how much to water, and a host of other gardening routines that can be better accomplished through the planning and calculating features of readily available home computer programs.

Not only will your computer save you time and money, it will allow you to pursue your gardening activities at the computer keyboard during those long winter evenings when your hands itch to feel the handle of a hoe. . . .

This 1,500- to 2,000-word article lists a variety of inexpensive home-computer software programs useful in managing a vegetable or flower garden. It shows how the gardener can gain valuable time to sow and reap by letting the computer accomplish the planning and preventive maintenance chores. It shows also how computerized gardening can become a teaching tool for a family, 4-H group or gardening club, covering the basics in both gardening and computer skills. And it shows an assortment of simple gardening aids I've developed over the past several years with the aid of my trusty PC.

That query, reports Patterson, "sold in three different versions to as many magazines. Needless to say, I updated the material and fine-tuned the query to meet the specific needs and readership of each magazine."

Many times you will choose not to offer even the minimal additional explanation provided by Patterson; this is especially true when there are many facets to your article. Indeed, you may decide the best way to show your plan for developing your proposed article is with a list, ticking off the individual discussion points one by one, with only a phrase or two of elaboration (or even none at all). Here's how free-lancer Carol Silverman Saunders previewed her article idea in a query that brought an assignment from *Parents* magazine:

> The feature I propose, "Is There a Gun in the House?" will include:
> - Examples of children hurt and killed by guns in the home, including the Brooklyn boy who last week shot his cousin while acting out a Nintendo scenario. I'll also cite statistics on accidental shootings and the number of guns in homes.
> - Examination of the concept, "Guns in homes are more likely to kill members of the household than to be used to confront an intruder."
> - How to make sure your child understands what real guns do. My six-year-old recently said, "Guns can't really kill anyone, Mom. They're just pretend."
> - What to make of children's gun play and toy guns.
> - Content of gun safety awareness programs being offered in some schools.
> - Information and quotes from the Center to Prevent Handgun Violence, the National School Safety Center, child psychologists, and, for balance, the National Rifle Association.

Saunders promises to cover a lot of territory in her article, and employing a list provided her an efficient means for making the promise. Her editor could easily see the breadth of Saunders's topic and the progression from one point to the next. (There's a visual benefit here, too: The six asterisks on the page provide a look that says, "This article will contain lots of information.")

It would be convenient to say that the complexity of your article determines when to elaborate on your proposal's main points. Convenient, but inaccurate. Even less complex articles can be outlined without additional comments. For instance, my in-laws article had few components, but I decided not to elaborate on either the strategy or the examples I promised to offer. Why? Part of the answer is the necessity factor mentioned above. I sensed that neither the strategy nor the examples needed to be explained further for the editor to understand their roles in the finished article. Since these explanations weren't necessary, I left them out. (Similarly, in Saunders's query, we don't need to know what the various groups' spokespeople will say to understand the role of their comments in the article. So Saunders was able to skip over previewing those quotes.)

But there was another rationale for why I chose not to elaborate on my outline: because the query felt complete without the additional comments.

Hardly a scientific answer, eh? But a great many of writing's decisions are made that way—by intuition, or guesswork, or flying by the seat of the pants. The thousand and one decisions a writer makes each time he sits down at the keyboard aren't governed by mathematical formulae. They are only informed by what you, the writer, have read, what you've done before, and whatever sounds right to that little voice inside your head. Which is why you do all that reading and all that writing and all that talking to yourself.

The in-depth outline

Intuition suggested to Sally-Jo Bowman that her first query to *Audubon* magazine needed elaboration. The result not only fully explores her topic and her slant, it also previews her writing style—and the compatibility of that style to *Audubon*. "The amount of detail, the use of quotes, and the literary style in the query are similar to what you'd see in the magazine," Bowman says. Here are the opening and middle of Bowman's letter, which resulted in an assignment to write the article she called "Trouble in Paradise":

"Welcome to Puna, the Pittsburgh of the Pacific," says Tom Luebben, an attorney who has been fighting since 1985 for the preservation of Wao Kele o Puna, the last sizable lowland rain forest in the U.S. It ranges over 27,000 acres on the flanks of Kilauea, the world's most active volcano. Luebben's nightmare of the future includes a forest desecrated with hundreds of geo-thermal wells and numerous power plants spewing the southeast section of the island with the toxic, rotten-egg stink of hydrogen sulfide.

Nonsense, says Roger Ulveling, director of Hawaii's Department of Business, Economic Development and Tourism. Geo-thermal development would take only 350 acres, and would free Hawaii from its current 90 percent dependence on oil. Currently True Mid-Pacific is drilling test wells in Wao Kele o Puna, and the state operated an experimental geothermal power plant outside the forest from 1981 until last year, when it was closed after a series of hydrogen sulfide accidents. But, Ulveling insists, "There is no hydrogen sulfide problem with the new technology. And the forest is likely to be dead in ten years anyway. We're requiring a forest management plan by developers, and that may save more of the forest than not doing anything. Without this, Hawaii island may have brownouts this year and blackouts next year."

Manabu Tagomori, deputy director of the Hawaii Department of Land and Natural Resources, dismisses growing opposition to development as mere "not in my backyard" thinking. But even state officials acknowledge that their adversaries have grown more troublesome since early this year when a small group of native Hawaiians called for help from national and international environmental organizations. Almost immediately two hundred who had demonstrated a few months earlier increased their ranks tenfold in a March of civil disobedience that resulted in 141 trespass arrests.

If developers paid heed to mythology—which a great many

Islanders do—they wouldn't fool with the fickle fire deity, Pele. Five years ago the goddess laid a blanket of lava over the first drill site. Now developers are drilling test wells downslope.

To some natives, the exact drilling location doesn't matter. They believe development is akin to exploring under the Vatican. "Pele isn't for sale. There is no compromise," says Noa Emmett Aluli, a Hawaiian physician. "We're not troublemakers," says native wood-carver Alapai Hanapi. "But we respect our ancestors' beliefs. Without those beliefs, we have no culture."

Experts disagree over the potential environmental effects on the rain forest. But it's possible that exploratory drilling could irrevocably harm the forest lands and then reveal geothermal resources insufficient or unsuitable for commercial development.

Resolution of the issue—which is of the magnitude and complexity of the old growth forests controversy in the Northwest— is likely to have heavy impact on the Hawaiian activist movement and on the international effort to save rain forests. Says Meg Ruby of Greenpeace, "It makes no sense for the U.S. to demand serious political changes and sacrifices of foreign leaders if we're not going to do it at home in Wao Kele o Puna, the most significant lowland tropical rain forest in the country."

Obviously, this is a longer query letter, as many of Bowman's are. "I figure," she says, "if I'm going to lose an editor, it will be in the first paragraph. On the other hand, I never go past two pages." A few editors bluster about the one-page limit to queries, but the majority recognize when a writer is being thorough and when he hasn't focused his idea.

This is also the most narrative example we've looked at; Bowman's query could pass for a short department article in many magazines. But don't be misled by the style of this letter and think that a piece of fancy writing will win over editors. Reviewing the narrative shows how Bowman previewed the "comprehensive investigative piece" she wanted to write.

The opening quote is grabbing and immediately suggests that Puna is the scene of controversy and confrontation. Bowman lets those ideas hang briefly while she provides a line of background information that also establishes Wao Kele o Puna's environmental importance—a critical point when trying to sell the editors of *Audubon*. Then it's back to the controversy as Bowman describes Luebben's nightmare.

By using Luebben's vision to describe the scene and prefacing it with the words "nightmare of the future," Bowman suggests her article will be sympathetic to the preservationist side of the controversy. This says, right from the start, that Bowman understands *Audubon*'s editorial viewpoint and which side the magazine's readers would likely be on. This is a small point and one that may seem obvious (I doubt *Audubon* would come to mind as a logical market for an article that had a "look at the progress environmentalists are stopping now" viewpoint), but this sort of intonation can raise an editor's comfort level when examining an idea from a writer she doesn't know.

This is also a point in which a little goes a very long way. And it's quite easy to go too far. Bowman is not explicit in her suggestion; it's a matter of word choice and positioning and, even, reading between the lines. What Bowman never does is allow the editor to think her article will be anything other than balanced and fair to both sides of the controversy.

We see this balancing in the next paragraph, with a state official explaining the project's benefits. There's more background here, too, this time related to the drilling in Puna. This is the letter's longest paragraph and deservedly so: The information is central to the Puna debate.

The third paragraph returns to the controversy surrounding the development plans, first with a state official dismissing the project's opponents, then with another bit of background that indicates the opposition may be growing. Bowman's statement about national and international environmental organizations' involvement in the issue tells the editors of *Audubon*—a magazine that circulates throughout the United States—that this is not a matter that only interests Hawaiians. Bowman later reinforces the notion of far-reaching interest in this issue.

In each of her paragraphs to this point, Bowman has taken a line or two to provide background information—background on what and where Puna is, on the development plans and past drilling, and on the protests so far. Some background information is essential to this query;

Bowman knows that this controversy isn't well known outside Hawaii and doesn't expect the editors to be familiar with its history. This is often a sensible approach to stories about relatively unknown or complex topics. The writer's task is to determine what background the editor *must* have and then deliver it effortlessly. (Writers face this same dilemma in writing articles, but the concern is magnified by the brevity of the query.) Rather than dumping her information all at once, Bowman spreads it over several paragraphs, mixing "new" and "old" information to maintain reader interest.

In her fourth and fifth paragraphs, Bowman introduces new dimensions to the controversy: mythology and native culture. Both of these aspects work to promise editors a better "story"—one that isn't just another feud in the struggle between development and preservation.

In the sixth paragraph, Bowman introduces her story's final dimension: the possibilities that the promised benefits don't exist and that even looking for them could do irrevocable harm to the rain forest.

By now editors have a grasp of the story. So Bowman uses the last quoted paragraph to give the controversy a higher profile. First, she compares it to the well-covered old-growth forest controversy raging in the Pacific Northwest. Then she enlarges the playing field by suggesting that *this* controversy's resolution will impact the *international* effort to save rain forests. Both statements carry a lot of sales appeal: the chance to be on top of the "next" big environmental fight and the chance to cover the important rain forest story from a new angle.

Strip away the narrative style of this letter, and Bowman has given *Audubon*'s editor an outline of her proposed article. Each paragraph talks about a different aspect of the article she proposes to write. As I commented at the beginning of this discussion, Bowman felt the detail, quotes and literary style of her query would help her gain the trust of *Audubon*'s editor, who was not familiar with her work. But style doesn't forgive substance. Had she chosen another path, Bowman could have promised the same article with this letter:

> There are no horned owls in the forests of Wao Kele o Puna, but development plans have ignited a Hawaiian debate that rivals the Pacific Northwest's in magnitude and complexity.
>
> Ranging over 27,000 acres on the flanks of the world's most

active volcano, Puna is being targeted for geothermal development that may free Hawaii from its dependence on oil. But environmentalists fear the cost of development may turn the last sizable lowland rain forest in the U.S. into the "Pittsburgh of the Pacific."

In "Trouble in Paradise," I'll examine the development plans and the opposition to them—opposition that has increased in recent months as national and international environmental organizations have come to the aid of local protesters. I'll also discuss the cultural concerns of native Hawaiians, who deplore the trampling of ancestral grounds, as well as the presence of Pele, the mythical goddess of fire who some Islanders suggest laid a blanket of lava over an early drill site.

The choices eventually made in this tropical forest will determine more than whether Hawaiians experience power brownouts predicted for the future. Leaders of Greenpeace and others suggest that the United States will lose its credibility to demand the sacrifices necessary to save rain forests elsewhere if it is unwilling to forego development in Puna.

This version is shorter than Bowman's actual letter by more than half. But it is simply a more compact version of the same outline she offered. I don't think it's a better letter, but I also don't think it's a bad one. It certainly doesn't have the style of Bowman's. Nor does it preview the topic (or the article on that topic) as completely. But for many topics at many magazines, this sort of outline would be enough to win an assignment. My letter also heeds the one-page taboo, but in the case of this particular query, I agree with Bowman's rationale for breaking the taboo: The unknown writer must work harder for an assignment. Bowman felt she needed to prove not only the quality of her topic for *Audubon*, but also her ability to organize such a multifaceted topic and the appropriateness of her writing for the magazine.

The narrative outline

Another time that a longer query letter might be appropriate is when you're proposing to tell a story—the type of article that's often called a narrative. The best narratives challenge writers to combine the storytelling techniques of fiction with the research and organization skills of nonfiction. But as tough as they can be to write, narratives can be even more challenging to query: This letter must convince the editor that you've found a compelling story to share with her readers, and you must do so in thousands of fewer words than you'll use in the article.

Freelancer Susan G. Fey knew she had such a story, one that "would warm the hearts of readers," as she said in the first line of her query to *Woman's Day*. Her second sentence opened her pitch by summing up the spirit of the story she proposed to tell. Then Fey moved into a condensed version of the story:

> Ideal for a winter 1995 issue, the piece would recount the story of a frozen city that warmed to a sick little girl's plight.
>
> When a record snowfall was dumped on Louisville, Kentucky, last January, the city was paralyzed. That was bad news for three-year-old Michelle Schmitt, who'd been on a waiting list for a liver transplant since she was a year old. On January 17, the day after the snow fell, Michelle's grandmother received the call for which the family had been waiting. By sundown a liver would be waiting for Michelle.
>
> In Omaha, Nebraska.
>
> But there was no way for the child to get to the airport. No way for pilots to get there. No way for planes to take off, with the airports closed. No way for emergency medical workers to get out of their driveways.
>
> A race was on, and Louisvillians responded to Michelle's predicament. Volunteers cleared a church parking lot so that a helicopter could pick up Michelle and her family and take them to the airport. A donated corporate plane, which had been readied for the trip, was able to make it to the runway only after the runway was cleared by more volunteers. That plane shuttled her to Omaha, where the transplant was performed.
>
> Months later, Michelle, who suffers from a liver condition known as biliary atresia, is all smiles. Her pudgy cheeks are the only outward sign of the transplant, a side effect of the drugs Michelle must take for the balance of her life to prevent her body from rejecting her new liver. Her prognosis appears good.

Although Fey would eventually use a thousand words to tell this story to *Woman's Day*'s readers, she needed only around two hundred and fifty to preview it for the editors. But in those five paragraphs of her query letter, Fey set the stage (snowed-in Louisville), named the conflict (no way to get to the liver), summarized the plot (the actions of the volunteers), and told how it all came out (happily every after). She told, in essence, the whole story.

(Too many beginning writers treat the query as a come-on, telling only part of a story in hopes of arousing the editor's curiosity. The notion is that the editor will ask to see the complete story, if only to find out how it ends. Bad move. What's aroused is the editor's irritation with unprofessional writers *and* her stack of rejection slips.)

Don't misunderstand me, though. Longer isn't always better. Not every article idea is a story that must be spelled out in detail. Not every magazine has the same tone as *Audubon*. And not every topic would support the in-depth previews these ideas did. The constant is this: Every query letter requires the writer to outline the scope of his proposed article. The question is how much elaboration do you provide with this outline? In these examples, Saunders provided none or only a single line for each point on her outline. Patterson ticked off examples but offered no real depth. Greco elaborated on one point, while letting the others stand alone. Bowman provided a paragraph on each, although the central issues of the debate received more attention than other dimensions. And Fey told her whole story, compressed into a page and a half.

The guideline is to give the editor enough to know she can trust you to complete the assignment with a complete, publishable article. Each of the writers above trusted his or her intuition (or marketing savvy or inner ear or whatever you choose to call it) to say how much was "enough." Practice will help you learn to do the same.

Essential ingredients

You can foster an editor's trust in your article-writing abilities by building into your sell copy some elements that demonstrate your professionalism. Not each of these will be appropriate in every query, but you should at least consider them as you write.

A working title

It always surprises me when a writer fails to give his proposed article a title. Can you imagine picking up a magazine and finding an article run without a headline? Would you even notice the article?

I suppose the writers of title-free queries assume that working titles are meaningless. After all, article titles are nearly always changed by the editors. That's true—but the assumption's logic is exactly backward. Editors—at least, *this* editor—change titles because we're looking for the best headline, the one that captures both an article's spirit and its topic's attractiveness to the audience. That may mean a headline that's straightforward ("Selling Your Poetry Collection," "Gift Books for Writers," "Six Workshops for Developing Playwrights"); or one that has a bit of a twist ("The Personal Essay Revealed," "Master Your Style," "Ordinary People—Extraordinary Sales"); or one that is almost mysterious ("Scripting the Company Line," which concerned writing corporate videos; "What's Screwing Up Your Characters?," which dealt with creating internal conflict in fictional characters). We change the headline in an attempt to attract more readers to the article.

Whether the editor's headline is better than the writer's working title is open to debate—but it's a moot one for this discussion's purpose. As a writer, you want to title your proposed article for the same reason the editor will put some headline on the edited manuscript: You want to attract readers (*a* reader, in your case). It catches the eye. It provokes curiosity. It previews the topic to be discussed. At the least, a working title helps convey your article's focus. My title "The Key to Getting 'In' With Your In-Laws" wraps up my promise by telling readers, "Here's the one thing you must know to get along with your in-laws." (In fact, *Modern Bride* kept most of the line, titling the published article "Getting In With Your In-Laws.")

A good working title can also convey atmosphere. Sally-Jo Bowman queried *Audubon* magazine with an article titled "Trouble in Paradise." Even though such a familiar phrase might be considered a cliché, it was particularly apt for an article proposal concerning a controversial geothermal well and power plant planned for America's version of Paradise—Hawaii.

Another strategy is to go for the word play. Maybe it's the magazine I work for, but I'm particularly partial to this type of working title.

(My preference might also reflect my belief that the writer who's not afraid to twist a word or a line for his own devices is generally a creative writer who also trusts his creativity.) I'm not alone in my fondness for the style either. The editor of a health magazine once told me that he was thinking about rejecting a query for an article on fitness trends in Great Britain when he thought of the headline "Fit Brits." Now, as a one-liner, that wouldn't rate so much as a rimshot in a comedy club. But the editor liked the phrase enough to assign the article that inspired it.

I don't advise depending on the generosity of an editor's inspiration. Spend at least some time looking for an intriguing title for your article. I liked the play on "in" in my in-laws headline. For my follow-up *Modern Bride* article, on how to cope when your spouse returns to school, I went for the chuckle: "Love Me, Love My G.P.A." The magazine took a different tact—one that I found even punnier: "Mastering the Challenge: My Wife, the Graduate Student." Creating these sorts of clever titles isn't brain surgery, but they can give your proposal a critical lift.

Projected length

This statement tells the editor how many words you believe your article will run. Mention it in your sell copy when you have a reason to. My in-laws article is an example of such a time. Prior to querying this article, I'd read a *Writer's Digest* market report on *Modern Bride*. One need the editor mentioned was for shorter articles. Checking *Writer's Market*, I learned that *Modern Bride*'s preferred article lengths were 1,500 to 3,000 words. So I purposefully mentioned in my query—in the first sentence of the sell copy, in fact—that I planned to write the article in 1,500 words. I mentioned the length for a purpose.

In general I think you'll have more luck if you propose to write your article on the short side, and for a couple reasons. The first is economic: The magazine industry is in a protracted ad page slump. There are fewer pages of advertising in magazines purchased today than there were five or ten years ago. Most magazines set each issue's total page count according to the number of ad pages sold (usually, publishers aim for certain percentages of ad and editorial pages—say, 50/50 or 60/40). Fewer ad pages therefore mean fewer editorial pages. Fewer editorial pages mean fewer articles.

Maybe. The editor who is faced with fewer editorial pages would prefer her readers not notice that they are getting less editorial product than they did last year. Nor does the editor want the newsstand browser to judge the publication as not having much to offer. So the editor tries to pack as much into each issue as she can. It's a bit of sleight of hand that requires only simple mathematics: In a space that will hold five 3,000-word stories, I can instead run seven 2,000-word stories and one 1,000-worder. Her readers will see eight stories (and most won't notice that the pieces are shorter), and she'll have eight features on the table of contents page to grab the browser.

The second reason to propose shorter articles has to do with your experience—or rather your lack of it. No matter how many articles you've published elsewhere, you are an unknown quantity the first time you approach me, an editor. Your idea may be perfectly targeted, your query may read wonderfully, and your clips may be terrific, but . . . well, you have no track record with me. I'm not certain I can trust you. So I give you an assignment for a shorter piece. Rightly or wrongly, shorter pieces are considered easier to write. They also leave a smaller hole to fill if the writer craps out. And, best of all (to me), they earn smaller fees than mega-tomes.

That last bit, about the smaller fees, is why most writers want to write as long an article as they can—especially if the magazine says it pays by the word. But once your foot is in the door, once you've sold a couple articles to an editor, you'll be in a better position to propose longer works (and demand the top rate for them, as well).

There is one possible danger in mentioning a length. Occasionally, a writer will send a query to pave the way for an already completed manuscript. In the course of the letter, such a writer might propose "a 2,300-word article"—which is, of course, the exact length of his manuscript. Editors who are leery of already completed manuscripts (some fear receiving a piece rejected by their competitors; others simply prefer material written to their specifications) will spot the too-precise length and automatically attach a rejection.

Place your idea within a department

Part of the magazine industry's trend toward cramming more text into fewer pages is to group short items together. These groupings are often called "departments," with each department having a specific theme

(Health, Nutrition, Fitness and so on). Sometimes the department is a single article, but the theme (and department name) carries over from issue to issue. These departments resemble columns, except the article is written by a different writer each time.

A close reading of your target market will tell you if such opportunities exist. Consider them carefully, because they often present the best breaking-in point at a magazine. Department articles are nearly always shorter than feature articles, so the logic is the same as I discussed above: Editors prefer to test new writers on shorter pieces.

I also think that when you earmark the story idea you're proposing for a specific department, you do more than hone in on the best breaking-in point; you also indicate that you've studied the magazine enough to know that there is such a department and that its focus would encompass your article. Such a statement warms an editor's heart. When a would-be contributor to *Writer's Digest* positions his idea for our Writing Life or Tip Sheet departments, I know that he has at least some familiarity with the magazine. That merits the query closer consideration than if a small idea best suited for Tip Sheet were pitched to me as a topic worthy of 2,000 words.

Writer Sally-Jo Bowman thinks such positioning is important enough to lead off her query. The first line of a query to *Wildlife Conservation* read: "Story idea for Conservation Hotline."

(You may gain an extra advantage if the department you target is new. I remember being tremendously impressed by one writer's query that mentioned a *Writer's Digest* department that had only appeared—if memory serves—two or three times. In fact, our requirements for the department had not yet been added to our writer's guidelines. But the writer's idea was perfectly targeted.)

Refer to a previous article

This is a trick somewhat similar to placing your idea within a department. This one differs by suggesting to the editor a model for how you will structure your article, as opposed to positioning your query on a particular page of the magazine.

Very few writers reinvent the wheel when they sit down to write. There are a handful of basic article structures out there, and writers return to them time and again. This isn't to be mistaken for a lack of creativity; creativity is how you arrange the words and sentences on those structures. But if you're writing an article on "Ten Tips for Making It Through the Holidays," no one will think you a hack for numbering each tip.

Likewise, many magazines use the same type of article from issue to issue. At *Writer's Digest*, our staple is the how-to article that follows a step-by-step fashion. Your study of back issues will reveal to you those types of articles commonly run in your target markets. Once you've identified those common structures, see if your topic can be written in that fashion. If so, mention it in your query: "I plan to develop the article along the same lines as John Doe's treatment of holiday stress in your December issue."

The idea, again, is to help the editor visualize your article in a favorable light. Here's the opening of a letter I received from writer Roy DeLaMar, who conjured up the image of one of my own *WD* articles:

> I enjoyed your recent cover story on the women's magazines. As a freelancer who has made of lot of sales to those very magazines, I agree that they can be lucrative. The piece also got me thinking about a particular niche within the women's magazine market that can be extremely profitable: the parenthood titles.

DeLaMar doesn't invoke my piece as a model, per se. But by mentioning the article, he raised the comparison in my mind. The suggestion I imply from such a statement is this: "I know the sort of article you like, and I think I can do something similar on a different topic." And, again, it shows familiarity with the magazine. It even means DeLaMar read the bionote at my article's end.

Flattery

Yes, flattery. I discussed this in chapter three, but I mention it here because it's an element at work in Roy DeLaMar's query. I'm not so blind that I don't see it. But there's not a writer—or editor—around who isn't pleased to see the words *enjoyed* and *agreed* connected to his work.

Flattery can be effective, when used subtly and sincerely. Writers are naturally drawn to those magazines that they read often. (If you aren't, you should be.) Even before you study these publications carefully, you already have an innate feeling for the editors' preferences when it comes to questions of slant and style. And I think it's foolish to not let the editor know that when you're writing her a query letter.

One danger in this, of course, is overdoing it. More than a sentence is probably too much. Another danger is that the idea you're proposing doesn't show any evidence of the intimate knowledge you claim. That's when you appear foolish, or worse, a liar.

This isn't a line to work into every letter. Or even many. But when it feels appropriate, by all means compliment the editor. Just avoid drooling.

Initial research

I discussed earlier how much research a writer needs to do before he sits down to write the query letter. You do this to verify your idea, to make sure that things really are the way you believe them to be, and to be certain that enough material can be gathered to make your slant work. If you're promising to name the top ten honeymoon spots in your area, it's a good idea to make sure there are at least ten to name.

But don't hide this work. Your initial research can help sell your idea to the editor. As it did for you, your initial research will help convince an editor that your idea is grounded in reality. Further, the names, dates, statistics, and other concrete information you place in your query will help the editor see you as a qualified writer worthy of her trust.

In her query on the proposed geothermal power plants at Wao Kele o Puna, Sally-Jo Bowman included specific dates and sizes, and quoted six people by name. In a section of the letter not included in the excerpt above, Bowman tells *Audubon*'s editor that she had previously written on this topic for a newspaper (and included a photocopy of that article with her query). All of this combined to leave an impression of a writer who held a firm grasp on the story she was proposing.

I once queried a video magazine on a roundup piece of movies whose story lines involved writers. My premise was that "In the past five years, 'the write stuff' has been hot stuff as far as Hollywood is concerned." To back up my claim, I mentioned nine films by title. I also wrote, "I've identified three dozen recent videotapes that feature writers among the movie's characters." That's far more trust inspiring than a less precise rationale, such as: "It seems I'm seeing more films featuring a writer among the characters."

In a proposal to *Writer's Digest*, James Daly offered to introduce readers to the "exciting new market" of computer game scripts. Three sentences helped convince me that Daly had explored the topic before he queried: "Computer games earned $7 billion in 1993. . . . Story lines can take more than fifty hours to complete. . . . A typical Hollywood screenplay may be 25,000 words; an interactive game script may be three times longer."

Don't confuse initial research with personal experience, however. You may be proposing an article on how to buy a used car, for instance, and drawing on your fifteen years' experience as a used-car dealer. You certainly will want to mention this personal experience to the editor (we'll discuss this point in the next chapter). But your query will be even stronger if you mention that over the past five years, state attorneys general reported a 15 percent increase in complaints against used-car dealerships for unethical practices. (In fairness to used-car dealers, I pulled that number from the air. My used minivan works just fine, thank you.)

That little statistic makes your query stronger for a couple of reasons. As regards the topic, you've shown the editor that people—her readers—are increasingly facing a dangerous situation when they step onto a used-car lot. Dealers play a variety of tricks to make bad cars look good so buyers pay more for them. You've said this is a potential problem for her readers. Then you've shown her a statistic that says, in effect, "You know that problem he mentioned? Well, it's getting worse."

The second benefit you gain from quoting that statistic concerns how the editor views you, the writer. Simply digging up the number shows you to be a writer who's not afraid of research, who knows how to validate an opinion. You could, after all, have made essentially the same point by writing, "More and more people are having their wallets vacuumed by unscrupulous used-car dealers." But stating that percentage increase and quoting the reputable source give credibility to your statement. And that gives credibility to your reporting skills. Further, you've shown you know how and when to use statistics, which speaks well of your writing skills.

Not every topic will lend itself to trotting out statistics. But more will than you might initially think. Are you proposing a first-person narrative about surviving as a single mother whose ex hasn't paid child support in three and a half years? Your query should mention that 62 percent of all divorced women never receive the full amount of child support payments they're awarded. Or will your article be the story of your child's battle with leukemia? Then your query should include the startling fact that twenty-eight thousand children die of that disease each year, making it the third most common cause of death for those younger than twenty-one. (Again, I've made up these stats, but you get the idea.)

As you plan your queries, look for outside sources to quantify the opinions on which you've based your idea. If none truly exist, that doesn't mean you're excused from doing preliminary research. My mothers-in-law query and article were statistic free (for whatever reason, state attorneys general don't collate such complaints). Yet, I needed to explore my suggestion for better in-law relationships: Did it work for me? For others? Did other people think it wise advice? Was the advice easy for others to grasp and apply? There are limits, of course; I didn't fund a university's sociology department to conduct a statistically valid research trial. But I bounced the idea off my wife and talked it over with a couple friends. I showed it around enough to decide whether it was valid or not.

Offer answers

There's another benefit of using the query letter to show off your initial research into a topic. Because you already checked into some of the important questions provoked by your slant, you can preview the answers you'll offer the editor's readers. This avoids trying to define your idea with the questions you'll try to answer in the article.

"This drives me crazy," *Glamour* editor Judith Daniels told Judy Mandell in a *Writer's Digest* article. "For example, the writer might say, 'What about the new marriage? Are women marrying younger? Are couples putting more emphasis on this?' I don't care about the questions. Whether or not this is a story depends entirely on the answers. If the writer hasn't gone to the trouble of coming up with some interesting statistics or an anecdote or a quote, if the writer can't tell me what the answer is or what the thesis is, I can't go ahead with this. This is not a story. This is just an idea in search of a story."

This hearkens back to our earlier discussion of outlining the article you propose to write. An editor already knows the questions her readers are likely to ask about a topic. What she wants from you are the answers to those questions, and the query letter is your first—and perhaps only—chance to prove you can deliver them.

Projected sources and accessibility

It's one of those letters that in later years I've wished I'd saved. The query writer's intent was to write an article for *Writer's Digest* on some aspect of writing (the topic isn't important). He proposed to offer the advice through comments from a half dozen or so best-selling writers, whom he named. It was an OK query, one that had enough going for it so that I was still undecided when I reached this line: "If I receive this assignment, please send along these writers' addresses so I might contact them for their advice."

Do you know why this line immediately triggered my left hand to pull a rejection slip from the drawer? Look at it through my eyes: What did my correspondent's request tell me?

First, it told me that the writer didn't know what the best-selling authors would say—even whether they would agree with his ideas about the technique or not.

Second, it told me that the writer didn't know these authors and hadn't lined up their cooperation for this article.

Third, it told me that this assignment—if I chose to make it—would be a crapshoot. The writer couldn't guarantee what the finished article would say or who he'd wind up quoting in it ("Biff Bartholomew, whose western was shot down by the editorial board at Ballantine, advises writers to . . ."). To editors, a crapshoot is a golden opportunity to pay a kill fee—the check that goes out when an assignment crashes and burns. If you're thinking like an editor, you understand why we try to avoid crapshoots.

This doesn't mean the smart writer avoids naming names in a query. In fact, the smart writer will tell an editor who he intends to use as sources. Such naming can help bring credibility to your idea and increase its appeal for the editor. Movie theaters use the same logic when they place the star's name on the marquee along with the film's title.

Sometimes the sources you name will be "generics." In my in-laws piece, I promised to "use examples from my own marriage and from others' " to show my idea in action. Carol Silverman Saunders's gun safety query offered quotes from three specific associations and "child psychologists." In such cases, it's the ideas that are being featured. In my case, it was only important for the editor to understand that the article's advice has been successful among people just like her readers. With Saunders's article, the editor needed to see that voices beyond the author's would be heard.

Other times, you will name specific people whom you'll interview on the topic. In Roy DeLaMar's query on writing for the parenthood magazines, he included this paragraph:

> For their expert advice, I'd speak to editors at the various parenthood books, including Anne Murphy at *Parents*, Freddi Greenburg at *Child*, and Christine Loomis at *Family Life*. I've worked with these people for years and would not have trouble getting interviews.

DeLaMar scores two critical bonus points in those two sentences. First, he lists three appropriate sources to comment on his topic. They are "appropriate sources" because they edit parenthood magazines and are familiar with freelancers' attempts to work in this market. (And three is a good number: Editors hate one-source stories, and DeLaMar will still have more than one source if any of the three is out of the country. And, says one of the oldest laws of reporting, someone is *always* out of the country.)

DeLaMar's second bonus point rings up when he mentions his access to these sources. Knowing that he's worked with these editors, I accept that he'll be able to deliver their words to my readers. I accept that he has access, so I believe he'll deliver on this promise.

Another way to tell the editor whose comments you'll include in your article is to quote them in your query. In his query on writing computer games, James Daly included these paragraphs:

> For writers [making the jump from writing films to writing games], that means abandoning the traditional linear script de-

sign. Instead, there must be multiple plot lines and endings. A typical Hollywood screenplay may be 25,000 words; an interactive game script may be three times longer. "A game player must be entertained for many more hours than a movie lasts," says Hal Barwood, a long-time Hollywood screenwriter who now creates games for Industrial Light & Magic.

There is also the creative challenge of adding personality and soul to previously flat two-dimensional characters. "We need to develop three-inch people that you want to spend a lot of time with," said [Mike] Backes, who recently penned the script for *Rising Sun.*

Later in the query Daly wrote, "I have already completed some early interviews with Backes and Barwood," so I could reasonably expect both writers to show up in Daly's finished manuscript. (If they hadn't, I would have had reason to be dissatisfied. But we'll talk about that down the road.) By including their comments in his query, Daly sent the message that Backes and Barwood would play a role in describing this opportunity to my readers.

In her query for "Trouble in Paradise," Sally-Jo Bowman employs the same technique. By quoting an activist attorney, two native Hawaiians, two state officials and a Greenpeace spokeswoman, Bowman demonstrated to *Audubon*'s editors that her piece would deal with several aspects of the Wao Kele o Puna controversy and be fair to both sides.

But what if your prequery research doesn't include interviews with your major sources? After all, didn't I say part of a query's purpose was to make sure a market exists for a story *before* you invest significant time in researching the article? True enough. Unfortunately, the short questions require a long answer.

First, as we've discussed, you *will* need to do some research prior to writing your query—if only to validate your idea's slant. As you tackle this preliminary digging, consider approaching a potential source for a fact-finding interview. You might not want to hit up the biggest star on your list, but perhaps someone you've dealt with on a previous article or someone you feel more at ease in contacting (a friend of a friend, perhaps, or someone who speaks extensively on the topic).

Such a fact-finding interview may yield better angles for your article in addition to pithy comments for your query.

Second, tell the editor whom you hope to interview for your article. This was DeLaMar's strategy in his query on the parenthood magazines. But how is this different from the writer who promised writing advice from several best-selling writers and earned my rejection as a result? Part of it is phrasing—DeLaMar didn't promise the editors would participate. Another part of the difference comes in showing an editor how you'll reach this source or why you believe this source will talk to you. DeLaMar told me he knew the editors. If your next-door neighbor is a world-renowned expert in the topic at hand, by all means mention that fact when you say you plan to include her comments.

If you don't have a personal relationship with your source, don't pretend. Begin by making your query as complete as possible without mentioning your sources. If I were querying an editor for a piece on reducing home-related stress, I might say, "In addition, I plan to contact Robert M. Bramson, coauthor of *The Stressless Home*, for his insights on setting goals, and Stephanie Culp, author of *Streamlining Your Life*, for her organization tips." I'm offering no guarantees in this sentence, yet I've indicated that I have a plan for making this a credible article. Still, I could make my case stronger if making a few more phone calls will allow me to add, "Both authors' publicists have promised their help in arranging these interviews."

For the freelancer in search of an assignment, it can be very tempting to promise the sun, the moon, and the ghost of Elvis Presley in your query. What editor wouldn't snatch up an article on "Settling Household Arguments" that featured advice from globe-trotting problem-solver Jimmy Carter. But unless you've already interviewed the former president or have a spot hammering nails next to him at a Habitat for Humanity construction project, you might settle for three family counselors and a family court referee.

Geography

This is a minor point, but one that separates experienced freelancers from the less so.

When you write, the easiest sources to locate are those who live nearby. That's fine if your market is local in its scope. I live near the

Ohio-Kentucky border; quoting local experts is acceptable when I'm writing for Cincinnati-area publications. If my market extends throughout Ohio or Kentucky or Indiana, then my bank of experts should pick up voices from other parts of the appropriate state. And if my market is a national magazine, then I must find ways to reach experts from throughout the country.

Some experts are geography free. Book authors, for instance. Their work is available almost anywhere, so their home base is usually unimportant. But what about my hypothetical "Settling Household Arguments" proposal—the one that I'm not promising to get Jimmy Carter's advice for? If it's headed for one of the national parenthood magazines, I'm going to go after family counselors from three different areas of the country and the family court judge from a fourth.

I'll do this through networking. Let's say my research began with a counselor I met at a Christmas party last year. I call her, and in the course of the conversation I ask her, "Who do you know around the country who's well-versed in this area and good at talking about it?" I might even explain that my editor will expect voices from around the country. The counselor gives me two or three names, each of whom give me another name or two when I ask them the same questions. When several people mention the same person, that's the sign of a well-respected expert. Ditto for when I ask them to recommend an innovative referee. Pretty soon, I've got a three-page long-distance bill and comments to pick and choose from.

How much of this you'll do before you query is a matter of personal taste. But mentioning that "I'll be contacting family counselors from around the country . . ." tells the editor once more that you're a writer who understands her needs.

Graphic support

The largest national magazines have art staffs that include everyone from a design director down to a photo researcher. Most magazines, however, aren't the largest national magazines. At *Writer's Digest*, for instance, an editorial assistant tracks down photos and other artwork in between filing correspondence and writing up check requests.

At midsize national magazines on down to weekly hometown newspapers, editors depend on freelancers to help locate the artwork that will run crop to margin with their words. And in most cases, who better to provide it? The writer is (the editor hopes) intimately exploring the topic. He's the one digging up information, collecting quotes, making contacts. If you look at photographs and artwork as one more bit of research, the request is perfectly in order.

You give your query letter an additional boost by addressing the editor's need right from the start. In a letter to *Family Motor Coaching*, Texas freelancer Donald Ray Patterson promised to send the finished article "complete with transparencies, photos and maps." Sally-Jo Bowman's "Trouble in Paradise" query includes this line: "Big Island photographer G. Brad Lewis has a variety of excellent transparencies available." In both instances, the writer answered one of the editor's questions—"How will I illustrate this?"—almost before it could be asked.

Notice that neither Patterson nor Bowman said they were sending the artwork with the query. Unless otherwise noted in *Writer's Market* or in the magazine's writer's/photographer's guidelines, editors *do not* want to find artwork in the same envelope as your query letter. Simply mention that you can provide photographs, transparencies, diagrams or whatever artwork you believe the magazine might want. (This is another area where studying the publication pays off: What kinds of graphics has the editor run with similar types of articles? Can you provide or arrange for this sort of artwork if your idea is accepted?) If the editor wants to see your artwork in advance, which is rare, she can ask for it.

If you're about to argue that you aren't camera equipped, I have two questions: So what? and Why not?

The lack of a camera shouldn't deter you from offering graphic support for your articles. You are still closer to the story than anyone at the magazine, which allows you to at least point out the best sources. You'll earn recognition as an editor's friend by securing black-and-white prints or color transparencies to send along with your manuscript.

Where do you turn for photographs? Sometimes you'll be able to point your editor to a photographer who has work on file (as Sally-Jo Bowman could) or is able to set up the appropriate shots on demand. If your article is a profile, your sources may be able to furnish photos or tell you who has snapped them recently. (Look to local newspapers or institutional newsletters.) Public relations agencies and departments generally stockpile photos of company officials, products, buildings, destinations, and most anything else related to the people or things they're charged with promoting. Generally, finding the proper artwork is a matter of using your imagination. An article on stretching prior to exercising might be illustrated by photographs from a running show or exercise machine manufacturer or diagrams from a sports medicine clinic. The writer of an article on child proofing your home might find appropriate art from drug manufacturers (childproof caps) or government agencies that deal with consumer safety issues.

You can become camera equipped quite easily. Good-quality photos are within the technical and financial reach of almost any freelancer. A 35mm camera and lens with automatic focus, exposure control and film advance now runs less than four hundred dollars, and photography classes are available at many adult education programs around the country. (The costs for such classes and even the camera—if it's used exclusively for your writing—are tax deductible.) You may never crack the pages of *National Geographic* with your lens work, but you'll likely get good enough results to help your words make it into print.

I can have it for you . . .

Remember the old game show *Name That Tune?* Two contestants tried to underbid each other in the number of notes they needed to identify a song melody ("I can name that song in three notes"). Usually it came down to some poor schmoe trying to guess which was the right song from among the forty-eight million songs that begin with an F and an A-sharp.

I think of that contest when I read in query letters, "I can have this article on your desk three weeks from receiving your go-ahead." This might be a personal prejudice, but I don't start a stopwatch every time I make an assignment and then penalize the writer for every hour the letter carrier is late three weeks and three days later. (The three days is for my assignment letter to arrive.) What tickles me is that quite a few writers think two or three weeks makes much difference in editing a magazine with a five-month lead time.

I've seen others suggest that promising a quick turnaround may help you win an assignment to fill one of those last-minute holes that crop up in magazine's editorial lineups. This logic (?) first supposes that your letter will cross the editor's desk within the same day—even hour—as the hole. It further supposes the editor will say, "Hey, I've got two weeks to put a publishable, edited article into this hole. I think I'll give to it this writer I've never worked with before!" I'm not sure which of those scenarios is less likely to occur. (I've also heard editors who weren't filling a hole remark, "If he can cover this ground in two weeks, he won't cover it well enough for me. I'll pass.")

So, ordinarily, I'd suggest leaving this line out of your query letter. If disaster has struck and I require an article in two weeks to fill a hole, do you want me to pass over your query because you said you needed three weeks? Of course not. Even if they honestly believe they need three weeks to complete an article, if an editor asks for the piece in two, most writers would skip a few lunches, shortchange a couple nights' sleep, and eat the Overnight Mail charges to have that manuscript there in one week and six days.

There are times when providing a time frame is appropriate, however. Perhaps a specific event plays a key role in your article—say the end of a university research project or a sporting event or a key source's return from sabbatical. In that case, it's proper to let the editor know this: "Because the results of a University of Kentucky study will influence the advice I offer, I would like to deliver the manuscript after the study's results are announced May 1. I do expect to see a preliminary report before then, so, barring major revisions in their findings, I can deliver the article by May 15."

But that's an exceptional case. If the editor normally allows two months for assignments to be completed, it won't matter if your letter says you can do it in three weeks. And if the editor wants the piece in three weeks and she really likes your proposal, she'll ask if you *really* need the two months you suggested in your letter. Maybe. But it's not a risk that I feel comfortable taking.

The middle section of a query letter is where you capitalize on the editor's interest, which you captured in your opening. In these paragraphs, you must convince the editor that the story you're proposing is a good one. You do this by outlining your unique slant on the topic, by demonstrating its usefulness to the audience, and by mixing in any other selling point that will cause the editor to look favorably on your idea.

This may require you to write several drafts—you're trying to squeeze a lot into a very few paragraphs, even as you worry about hitting the right style and tone. Write them all, for each will help you address the editor's final question to every query writer: Why you? The first two sections of your letter have addressed that question indirectly, by showing off your creativity and your writing ability. The conclusion of your letter is where you answer it directly. We'll look at how to do it both gracefully and forcefully in the next chapter.

CHAPTER SIX

Ending Your Letter

You've grabbed the editor with a provocative opening. You've hooked her with a well-developed outline of an intriguing take on an area of interest to her magazine's readers. The only task remaining for your query letter is to sell yourself.

Oh.

This is the part of the query letter that newer writers fear most. They seem to trust their ideas—that is, they believe the ideas are ones the editors will be interested in—but they don't trust themselves. At least, they don't trust their credentials.

That's a healthy concern. Every editor asks at least two major questions in considering a query letter: Why this idea? and Why this writer? The middle section of your letter, which we discussed in the last chapter, is designed to answer the Why this idea? question. How to answer the second question is our topic here. Your goal, simply put, is to show the editor that you are the best person to write the article you're proposing.

The résumé

The final section of your query letter has much in common with the résumé you write to find a new job. A résumé is where you want to tell a prospective employer why you are a qualified candidate for the company's open position; in fact, you want her to believe that you are the *most* qualified applicant. You highlight your relevant experience, and you explain those accomplishments in your past that demonstrate your ability to perform the tasks of this open position.

To present the best image, you do not mention that you were fired from your last job for making a pass at the boss's wife during the Christmas party or how you drove over a customer's mailbox when delivering pizzas during your final year of college.

You should do much the same in the final paragraphs of your query letter. Mention the names of the magazines in which you've published, the names of books you've written and sold, positions within the publishing industry you've held.

For instance, Donald Ray Patterson included this paragraph in a query to *Family Motor Coaching*:

> My publishing credits include more than five hundred nonfiction article sales to national and regional consumer, trade and technical publications. My nature and travel articles have appeared in *Living off the Land, Well Being, Coleman Annual, Camperways, Camping Journal, Northeast Outdoors, Southern RV, Family Motor Coaching, Healthways, Camping Canada Magazine,* and *RV West.* I've also written and produced several multinational industrial newsletters, a dozen employee motivational film and video programs for industry, and a lecture series for Florida's Brevard Museum.

Here's James Daly's "résumé" paragraph from his query to *Writer's Digest*:

> I am a senior writer for *Computerworld* newspaper, a leading journal of the high-tech industry, and have worked as a freelance contributor to such publications as the *San Francisco Chronicle, Forbes, Spin* and *Billboard.*

And, finally, here is Carol Silverman Saunders in her query to *Parents*:

> My work is forthcoming in *Woman's Day, Good Housekeeping* and other magazines. My agent is shopping my book, *Safe at School.*

But what of the newer writer? What do you do if you can name no magazines you've sold to, no publishers who have paid you for the novel that even now rests at the bottom of the desk drawer (third one down, on the left)? And, except for a short stint as a fifth grader delivering newspaper, you've never held a job in publishing?

The good news is that editors base their decisions to use specific writers on more than previous writing experience. This is yet another area where I can quote the old adage, "Write what you know." Life experience with a topic is a credential you should mention when telling an editor who you are. Such life experience might take various forms: Your familiarity with the topic might be a result of:

- on-the-job experience (a used-car salesperson, for instance, writing about how to get the best deal on a used car or an appliance repairman offering tips for making the most common household repairs);
- educational training (a physical therapist offering exercise tips or a communications researcher writing about interviewing skills);
- personal hobbies (a Civil War enthusiast writing about the five most interesting battlesite monuments or an avid skier on the best new equipment);
- other special interest (a PTA volunteer offering tips on organizing more successful fund-raising drives or a literacy volunteer on one student's struggle to overcome her obstacles); or
- fate (the native of Florida writing on how the character of the state has changed or a flood victim offering tips on how to deal with insurance companies).

However you gained this experience, the editor knows your article will be richer and more compelling because of it. The flood victim can speak more authoritatively about the frustrations of insurance bureaucracies than the writer who has simply researched the issue. The skier's opinions of a new style of ski boot will mean more to a reader than someone who has only read the promotional brochure. The used-car dealer accumulated his tips and stories as he sat across the desk from real-life consumers.

And because of your intimate knowledge of the topic, the editor will be more likely to trust you with an assignment.

Does this mean you will be stuck writing only about those topics that you have some personal experience with? Probably not. One of the reasons editors tend to shy away from newer writers is because of their inexperience: Newer writers' research skills and writing styles are not as developed as those of more experienced writers. But newer writers can compensate for these "deficiencies" by proposing topics that they're experienced with. Editors know this familiarity will require the writers to do less research (which means less chance for error), and the depth of personal knowledge they'll bring to the assignment will compensate for a less-polished writing style. As your writing prowess matures, however, editors will begin to see you as someone with the research and writing skills necessary to craft a thorough and informative article on a topic that was—before the assignment—unfamiliar to you. It's a progression that eventually allows you to write about what you *want* to know, as well as what you already know.

In the last chapter, I quoted at length from a query that freelancer Sally-Jo Bowman sent to the editors of *Audubon* magazine. At the time, Bowman hadn't written for *Audubon*, so she crafted a query that mirrored the magazine's literary style to show her ability to write for that market. After outlining her plan for the article, Bowman tells the editor that she's already written on the controversial Hawaiian geothermal development issue for a newspaper in her home region. She then goes on to describe another credential, a special experience that only she can bring to the article:

> I am one-fourth native Hawaiian. I grew up on O'ahu. Although I live in Oregon, I go "home" often and do at least one freelance project each year on a Hawaii topic. My extensive personal and professional ties give me special entree into the Hawaiian community, which is often wary of "outsiders," especially if they are writers. But I am also sufficiently detached from Hawaii to delve into all sides of the issue.
>
> My current work includes a profile in the November issue of *Honolulu Magazine* and a feature on open adoption scheduled in *Family Circle*.

Bowman's query is strengthened by her publication credits. And even the credits she names speak to her credentials to write the piece she's proposed. The *Honolulu Magazine* article reemphasizes her Hawaii connection, and the *Family Circle* article shows that Bowman can write on complex, controversial topics.

Even when you have names of magazines to drop, you're credibility will be stronger if you tailor that information to reflect the idea you're proposing. In another query proposing a story with an environmental theme, Sally-Jo Bowman began her final paragraph, "My work on environmental topics has appeared recently in . . ." Similarly, in the final section of Roy DeLaMar's query on writing for the parenthood magazines, he highlighted his experience on both sides of the keyboard with the topic. After promising to interview editors in the field, he continued with this paragraph:

> I'd also draw on my own experience: I was an editor at *Parents* for nearly three years. And as a freelancer, I have written on parenthood topics for numerous magazines, including *Family Life, Target the Family, First for Women* and *Bride's*.

JoAnn Greco used the same approach in her query to *Writer's Digest* on writing about the trade magazines:

> My trade writing has appeared in *Billboard, Back Stage, Publishers Weekly, Video Store, Commercial Realty Review, Profiles in Healthcare Marketing, Lapidary Journal, Media & Methods, The NonProfit Times, Foundation News, Imprint* and others.

If you lack publication credentials of any sort, your final section must rest solely on experience. (Or you might skip it altogether—an option we'll discuss farther on.) One of my earliest query letters was to a city magazine, proposing to write an article called "Power Complaining." In the query, I promised to "guide would-be complainants to the right targets: to the people most capable of reading—and acting on—their complaints" and to "offer advice on how to write letters of complaint that get results." But I could cite no previous publication credentials (and I was too young and stupid—there, I said it first—to mention that I was an editor at *Writer's Digest*). So I established my credentials by relating a personal experience with a complaint letter:

> I've been a devoted letter writer since a calm, reasoned (rule #1) complaint letter brought an apology from the head of [a local hospital] and a reprimand down on an anesthetist who didn't

take the impending birth of my daughter as seriously as my wife and I needed him to. I look forward to helping your readers discover what I found: Revenge is sweet, but vindication is *so* satisfying.

The whole-letter résumé

All of these writers I've quoted so far have used the final paragraphs of their queries to help the editor trust them as writers experienced in the topics they were proposing. This isn't a notion restricted to the final section of the query, however. When appropriate, your entire query can serve as your résumé—even as you capture the editor's attention and outline your idea.

In the last chapter, we discussed highlighting your personal experiences concerning a topic. For instance, in my query letter to *Modern Bride* regarding in-laws, I promised "to use examples from my own marriage and from others' to show the strategy in action." But sometimes your personal experience will form the framework on which the query is built. The writer and the topic become almost inseparable. Here's the entire text of a letter I received from John Calderazzo. It was his first query to me, and it arrived with a book. Granted, the instant credibility of a book isn't a quality that many writers can give their queries, but Calderazzo doesn't depend on it. Note how he connects himself to the topic at every step:

> Dear Mr. Clark:
>
> Why recycle only aluminum cans and newspapers? Why not words? Like the words in that story that took two weekends to research and ten nights to write. The story you sold to your local newspaper for a fee that barely covered the cost of computer ribbon.
>
> It's ecological, in a way. Unless you've found a way to live forever, you can't afford to waste finite resources like time, energy and enthusiasm on just one sale. This is doubly true if you're a slow writer. I'm sometimes ridiculously slow, yet by teaching myself to reslant and resell my meticulously crafted stories, I learned to thrive as a full-time freelance writer.
>
> And I owe it all to boomerangs. . . .

I want to write an anecdotal article for *Writer's Digest* that will show how I published four versions of a feature story on the wacky topic of boomerangs. With lots of examples, I'll focus on the writing itself, the slanting and reslanting, particularly in leads. The stories appeared in *Ohio Magazine* ($450 for a piece that took me more than two weeks to produce), *Marathon World* ($1,000 for just a couple of more days' work), *Chevy Friends* ($400 for another few hours), and *Quest* ($200 more).

I'll adapt the article—mainly, scrunch it down—from one of the later chapters in my enclosed, newly published book, *Writing From Scratch: Freelancing. . . .*

Though I'm no longer a full-time freelancer (I'm an associate professor of English in [Colorado State University]'s creative writing program), I've published more than one hundred essays and articles in publications like *USA Today*, *Miami Herald Tropic*, *The Runner*, *Audubon* and elsewhere. And, in case you're wondering, I *have* gotten faster.

Sincerely,

This sort of résumé-in-every-paragraph approach is particularly well-suited to writers without publication credits to name. The danger is to make sure the editor recognizes that you're proposing something more than a retelling of your experience. Although Calderazzo is proposing "an anecdotal article" about publishing four versions of a feature story, notice that he doesn't introduce himself until deep in the second paragraph ("I'm sometimes ridiculously slow"). Before he turned the spotlight on himself, Calderazzo sold me on the importance of the topic ("you can't afford to waste finite resources like time, energy and enthusiasm on just one sale"). And, even as Calderazzo discussed his personal experience, he acknowledged my magazine's how-to slant (and my readers' need for instruction): "With lots of examples, I'll focus on the writing itself, the slanting and reslanting, particularly in leads." I knew I could trust this author to tell a story that my readers would appreciate (we'd all like to earn two thousand dollars-plus from a single idea) *and* learn from.

"I've enclosed clips . . ."

Supporting the publication credentials you list in your letter should be a few "clips," which is publishing jargon for photocopies of your previously published work. (You might also hear them referred to as "tearsheets.")

Clips give editors a chance to see more of your writing style and your ability to write an article—from lead to conclusion. Some editors won't make an assignment without first reviewing the author's clips; others may only consult them if the query alone didn't convince them. If you have good clips to send, send them—even if an editor doesn't directly request them in her *Writer's Market* listing.

You may be thinking that *any* clip is a "good" clip, but there are bad ones. I've seen them. And a bad clip can dissuade an editor from making an assignment she otherwise would have made.

What constitutes a good clip is, first, the overall quality of the article. Bad articles do occasionally get published, and even the least self-critical writer recognizes that some pieces don't show his talents at their best. And (I confess on behalf of my colleagues) an editor will occasionally trash a piece when she should have been editing it. Your story may have appeared in the most prestigious magazine in the world, but if you believe the editor botched the editing, don't send it out as a clip.

(What if the reverse were true: If your work was heavily worked over by an editor and—gasp!—made better for the rewriting? Minor revisions aren't a concern. But when an editor changes a substantial amount of your manuscript, I think it's a bit dishonest to send out that article with future queries. I read clips as the query writer saying, "Here's a sample of what I can do for you." So an article that actually reflects another editor's work isn't helping me judge your talent. And I will figure it out when your article arrives bearing no resemblance to the clip.)

A good clip is also one that shows how you handle articles that are somehow similar to the one you're querying. This similarity might be in topic or it might be in style. For instance, if you're querying a profile of a medical researcher, you might include in your clips a previously published profile on someone in another field and an information piece on medical technology. The two articles show the editor that you can write profiles and you can write on medical topics. Taken together, they suggest you can probably be trusted to write a profile about a personality involved in medicine.

Sometimes you'll be able to show more than just a similarity. With her query regarding the controversial development plans for a Hawaiian rain forest, Sally-Jo Bowman included a copy of a newspaper article she'd written on the same topic. This gave *Audubon*'s editor an immediate insight into what sort of article Bowman would likely write for that magazine.

As important as clips are to some editors, no one wants to see your whole portfolio. A single article can support your credibility quite nicely, and you should never send more than three. (If an editor needs to see more, she can request additional clips. But that's very rare.)

Your clips should reflect your professionalism. The photocopies should be crisp and clear—they're worthless to the editor if they aren't readable. Stick to 8½″ × 11″ paper whenever possible, but it's OK to load up 8½″ × 14″ sheets to accommodate newspaper features. The only acceptable colors are black ink on white paper. For magazine features, copy the full page. If the piece ran around ads over several pages, feel free to cut off the ads and condense the text onto a fewer number of pages. Two-sided copying of your clips is both acceptable and environmentally correct. (Clips only, however. Always use two sheets of paper for a two-page letter.)

Including clips not only helps establish your ability to write the article you're proposing, it also increases your potential of making a sale. It doesn't happen frequently, but a number of freelancers have told me of editors buying reprint rights to an article sent as a clip or even assigning a new treatment of a topic dealt with in a clip.

Help for the inexperienced

I sometimes think that the biggest injustice in freelancing is that the best query letters are required of those writers least prepared to write them—the inexperienced. Editors who aren't familiar with your work must find in your query letter their validation for making an assignment. Some editors are more forgiving than others, of course, but all will demand a well-written letter before making an assignment.

Inexperienced freelancers often make the task facing them harder by pointing out their inexperience—even apologizing for it.

> I've not written for a national magazine before, and I doubt if you're familiar with the local newspapers that have published my letters to the editor. . . .

I sold a few pieces when I was younger and, now that my children have gone out on their own, I'm looking forward to restarting my writing. . . .

I'm hoping you will be the first editor to publish one of my articles. . . .

Everyone in my writer's group says I should send out my work, so I thought I'd start with you. . . .

I'm seventy years old and figure it's never too late to start writing. . . .

I'm sixteen years old and my English teacher says I should be a writer. . . .

And so on. Unless you're directly asked, never admit to an editor that you're not completely familiar with working in whatever league you're querying in. I said back in chapter two that although I consider myself a competent writer, I don't believe I'm ready for *The New Yorker*. But when I decide I am ready, I can guarantee my first query letter won't let on that I consider this a milestone of any sort.

You must do the same. Don't apologize for your inexperience—in fact, don't even acknowledge it. Approach every editor as a professional, as a writer asking for an assignment. Craft the best letter you can, and let your writing speak for itself.

I said it earlier, and I'll say it again: You will improve your chances of gaining that assignment by proposing ideas that arise out of your personal experience. "Write what you know," remember? Then, don't sell yourself short. If you've been a classroom teacher for even a couple years, you know more about how parents can help their children do better in school than I—a (fairly) typical parent—will ever know. Unless you tell me. If you've worked in a department store for even six months, you can pass along tips for getting the best bargains that will delight even the most dedicated mall walker. If you've run the PTA carnival for a half dozen years, you have a storehouse of organization tips that will assist organizers of all stripes—amateur and professional. In each case, all it will take (in addition to a well-developed outline of what your article will say) is a comment along these lines: "In passing along this information to your readers, I'll draw on my experience as a second-grade teacher/a sales associate/the organizer of an all-volunteer corps of about thirty parents who stage a school carnival that annually raises in excess of twenty-five thousand dollars."

Freelancer Irwin W. Fisk had a few publication credits when he approached *Writer's Digest* with a query on a new interviewing technique developed for police that, said Fisk, would "also become the standard for journalists, writers and researchers." Fisk didn't rely on his credentials, though. His query included this paragraph, which any first-time writer could adapt when proposing an article that grows out of personal knowledge:

> As a law enforcement investigator, I used CIT [Cognitive Interviewing Technique] regularly to draw out details from witnesses. As a writer, I first used CIT when interviewing a ninety-nine-year-old woman for an article on the 1906 San Francisco Earthquake that I was writing for the *Los Angeles Herald Examiner*. The first interview lasted nearly two hours, and she remembered the events in a very general way, but the interview yielded few details. I scheduled another interview, and this time, using CIT, she recalled several vivid scenes that I used in the story.

All of your experiences count for something. Once you decide what they are, don't forget to clue in the editor.

"Don't I know you?"

There is one experience that you should be sure to note in your query letter: if you've met the editor at some time. Such a meeting might occur in any number of ways, of course—from a chance meeting at a cocktail party to an arranged interview for some other article. (It's happened before: Reporters have called me for comments on some writing-related topic. Two weeks later, there's a query on my desk.) Most commonly, though, writers meet editors at the various writers' conferences held each year throughout the country. These sessions have much to offer a writer, including the chance to pick up specific tips directly from editors you might like to write for.

(Among the better opportunities are the conferences sponsored by *Reader's Digest* in conjunction with a local university's journalism program. These two-day programs feature eight to twelve editors speaking about the editorial needs of their specific magazines—including *RD*—

with plenty of opportunities to speak with them one-on-one. Also valuable are the annual American Society of Journalists and Authors conferences in New York City and Los Angeles, which bring together writers and editors on panels devoted to specific types of writing. However, the opportunity to meet privately with an editor for even five minutes at an ASJA conference is rare. A list of writers' conferences appears each year in the May issue of *Writer's Digest*.)

If you send a query letter to an editor after such an event, by all means mention it in your letter. This is true even if you didn't actually speak privately with the editor. "I attended your helpful talk at the Midwest Writers' Workshop. I believe this query responds to the need for first-person narratives you mentioned." Or, "I appreciated your discussion of interviewing techniques at last fall's Golden Triangle Writers' Conference. Since then I've had several occasions to use your tips on getting answers from reluctant subjects." Or even something like this extract from Susan G. Fey's query to an editor at *Woman's Day*:

> Incidentally, we met in 1989 at the *Reader's Digest*/University of South Carolina Department of Journalism and Mass Communications Magazine Writers' Workshop. I told you then I'd never give up sending story ideas to you, and it looks as if I'm true to my word.

As I said in regards to flattery, sincere appreciation for an editor's comments or time is always welcomed. It won't necessarily help your case—and it won't turn a "no" into a "yes"—but it will almost certainly gain your query a slightly closer reading. And closer, as the commercial suggests, really is better.

The final statements

One of the cardinal rules of advertisement writing is to "tell the reader what to do next." That may sound sort of silly—after all, why else would you be telling someone about your product unless you want them to buy it? Nonetheless, research shows that response increases when you say, "Call us today for a free estimate" or "Drop the enclosed card in the mail to reserve your new edition" or "Stop by and buy yours today."

Now I won't tell you that your target editor won't know what to do if you end your letter without asking for the assignment. I really believe just about all of my editor colleagues are sharp enough to tell a query letter from *Newsweek*'s latest subscription offer (at our preferred "professional rate!"). But such a line is also a graceful way of ending your letter.

> I look forward to your interest in running "Trade Off."
> —*JoAnn Greco*

> Thank you for your consideration. I look forward to hearing from you soon.
> —*Roy DeLaMar*

> If you would like to discuss this idea further, I can be reached at (555) 555-0000. Thanks for your consideration. I look forward to hearing from you soon.
> —*James Daly*

> I'd like to write "Trouble in Paradise" for *Audubon*. May I have the assignment?
> —*Sally-Jo Bowman*

In my own queries, I often use a "thanks for your consideration line," but sometimes not. It's a matter of pacing, flow, length, and whether something better has occurred to me. I do believe a thank-you is in order, though, just as you expect to hear (or even see) "Thanks for stopping by" when you leave a merchant. The editor has given you a piece of time to consider your proposal. It's appropriate to say "Thanks."

And that's it. You've composed a beginning, a middle and an end. As with any good story, that's enough. All that remains is a complimentary closure (*Sincerely* or *Respectfully* work just fine) and your signature.

But is your letter ready for the editor's critical view? Before you type up your final draft or execute the "type" command, read it once more. This time, read it as your target editor will, bearing in mind everything you've learned about the magazine and its preferences. In the next chapter, we'll look at some finer points of the process, including whether you should send this letter to more than one editor at once. Then in chapter eight, we'll examine what will happen once your letter reaches its destination—including why the editor will hunt for a reason to tell you "no."

CHAPTER SEVEN

Other Forms of Queries

The plan for writing a query that I discussed in chapters four, five and six will serve you for most types of queries. As I showed in chapter five, the middle section of your query can be as long or as short as seems necessary to preview the article you're proposing. You can briefly list the main points you'll cover or you can expand each of those point into a full paragraph. It is a versatile format.

But there are circumstances that call for other types of queries. This chapter will look at those, as well as some of the options you have for delivering your idea into the editor's hands.

The multiple idea query

This is a query I strongly recommend you not send on your first submission to a particular editor—no matter what your publishing track record is. Wait until you've sold one or two articles to an editor. Those couple of sales give you a track record with the editor. She knows what you're capable of, how thoroughly you complete an assignment, how well you understand her audience—in short, she knows what she can expect from you.

The Multiple Idea Query trades on that familiarity. In it you present two, three or four different article ideas. (More than four gets to be awkward.) Unless you want to wreck your fledgling relationship with this editor, you must still carefully mold each idea to the magazine's readership. The difference comes in presentation. When querying multiple ideas, you don't need to outline each idea in the depth you do when knocking on an editor's door for the first time.

The opening paragraph of this letter is an excellent place to take care of old business, to compliment the editor on how your last piece looked in print, or to simply thank her for some recent correspondence. If it's been more than, say, six months since you've crossed her desk, you might use the opening to remind the editor of your past contributions. End this paragraph with a sentence along these lines: "I have a few new ideas that I hope you'll find appropriate for your readers."

Separate each idea by running its working title as a subhead (much as the words "The Multiple Idea Query" appear above). You can print that line in boldface type if you're still trying to justify spending so much on your laser printer, but quote marks or underlining will do just fine otherwise.

Under that headline, briefly describe your article idea. Keep your description to the essentials: the topic, the hook and a glimpse of what you'll say. If you've found an eye-catching anecdote, use it. The same goes for compelling statistics and quotes. Mention, too, any personal experience you have with the topic. Just make sure everything works to help the editor see the article you're proposing. Even more than in a single-article query, there's no room for tangents and asides.

After you finish one idea, skip a space and type the working title for your next proposal.

When you've described all your ideas, skip a space and close your letter with a shortened version of the résumé section I described in chapter six. This is an excellent opportunity to update the editor on your most recent publications: "Since my last piece in *Writer's Digest*, I've sold articles to *Woman's Day* and *Parents*."

It is unlikely that a multiple idea query will bring multiple assignments. Depending on the editor and your past relationship with her, you may get a go-ahead or a request for more details on how you'd develop a particular idea. (Or you might get a multiple rejection. Isn't freelancing fun?) If you receive an assignment on the basis of a shortened query, you might want to call the editor to discuss your plans further—"just to make sure I'm heading in the right direction."

Occasionally an editor will express interest in more than one of your letter's ideas, even though she only makes one assignment. Make note of that interest, so you can return to the idea when the assigned piece is completed and accepted. The best way to remind the editor of her past interest is to photocopy her original letter and attach a note along these lines: "If this idea still appeals to you, I'm ready to write it. I look forward to hearing from you."

The business proposal

I must admit that I don't really understand this approach, but I see it recommended often. So I include it for completeness's sake. The business proposal comes in two parts: a cover letter and a separate article proposal. I'm sure there are times when this approach is particularly appropriate, but I haven't run into them. But I do see this format frequently. (I don't reject such proposals out of hand, mind you; I just don't see the point in separating the parts.)

In the cover letter, the writer introduces the topic of the article, refers the editor to the attached proposal, and states his credentials. The second-page proposal "sells" the idea, using the same techniques I discussed in chapter five. Because the format dictates a two-page presentation from the outset, you must keep your proposal to a single page. Perhaps this is why the writing in these proposals tends to be more straightforward, more businesslike, but it's not a requirement of the form. My guess is this format has its roots in business reports and proposals and inherited some of its ancestors' style. But the editor will still be judging this letter as a writing sample, so attention to tone is critical.

Use this format if it makes sense to you—or seems appropriate to your target market.

The letter of introduction

This is a letter reserved for writers who can boast substantial track records in their target markets. In this letter, the writer introduces himself to an editor and recaps his experience in the magazine's field of interest. The letter may or may not offer a specific article; mostly it's a fishing expedition in which the writer invites the editor to call him with assignments that seem appropriate.

The Letter of Introduction is always accompanied by clips or, per-haps, a book on a topic related to the magazine's field of interest. This letter is the perfect format for suggesting an editor consider running an excerpt from your book. Or, "If none of the book's chapters strikes you as right for your audience, I'd be happy to discuss any topics that you believe might fit my expertise."

The column proposal

If you work for and study a magazine long enough, you will want to carve out a regular piece of it for yourself. You can accomplish this in one of two ways: Steal the editor's job or propose a column.

The first idea is a matter for some other book. Proposing a column, however, requires you to send a special query.

It's not imperative that you have written for a magazine before pro-posing a column. (It's helpful, certainly, but not a requirement.) What you must have is a great deal of practical experience in the topic you want to write about. For instance, selling one novel wouldn't rate you a shot at *Writer's Digest*'s Fiction column. The current writer of that column has published a half dozen novels and a score of short stories. But she'd only sold *WD* two articles—one of which we invited—before she won the column assignment.

Your column proposal should follow the Business Proposal format outlined above. Begin with a letter that directly communicates your interest in a column-writing assignment and describes the hook that will make your column distinctive from others in the magazine. (If you're making a grab for another writer's column, you got guts. And you better have a great new hook, too.) Work on this initial statement until it sings; it must be both compelling and descriptive.

In this letter, don't go into detail about your plans for the column. Make your pitch, refer the editor to your attached material for more details, and move on to the section that will make or break your pro-posal—your credentials. Your target editor wants to see an expertise born of a real-life familiarity with the topic that's been bred with exten-sive writing experience. If you were proposing, say, a nutrition column for a fitness magazine, the editor would expect you to possess some sort of dietary or other human science background, as well as a history of writing on the topic from an exercise perspective. Spend time on this résumé, listing as many credits as you can legitimately claim.

Close your letter with an invitation to discuss the column further. If you are able to visit the editor, offer to meet at her convenience.

The second piece of your proposal should be a detailed description of the column. Define its topic and what benefit readers will get from it. Will the column attract new readers to the magazine, and who will they be? Justify your column's place in the magazine. You might even place yourself in the editor's chair and suggest an existing feature you'd jettison to make room for your column and why this change would make for a better editorial package. This is certainly a brash tactic (some might say presumptuous even), but this is not a time to waffle or tread lightly. You're asking for a page or two in every issue to express your opinion: Your reasons must be solid.

After you describe the column, show the editor how you'll develop it. Put together a lineup of column topics for the first year (two years if the magazine is published less frequently than monthly). This list should illustrate that you are creative enough to make this hook come alive month after month without repeating yourself.

Finally, choose one of the topics from your lineup and write a sample column. Don't make it the piece that introduces the column to readers—you'll just end up repeating your proposal's description. Pick a topic that allows you to burrow into the column's soul and demonstrate why readers will love your approach, your voice and your advice.

Round out your package with a selection of clips, favoring those articles that best display your style and your command of the subject matter. For this type of package, six to eight clips is not too many.

The reprint offer

The most effective marketing a writer can do—in terms of dollars earned for time spent—is to sell reprint rights to your published articles. Your first step will be to search *Writer's Market* for those magazines that accept reprints. (Also check sample issues for credit lines that indicate material picked up from other sources.)

Your best targets will be magazines that don't compete with your original market, but still have an interest in your topic. For instance, let's say your article on successful tactics for recruiting church members was published in a magazine sent to Presbyterian church leaders.

The methods you describe aren't specifically Presbyterian, yet it's unlikely that Methodists or Lutherans would have seen them. Magazines serving those denominations—or any other denomination—would be likely reprint markets. You can offer reprints in several ways:

• *Recycle your original query letter.* You must revise it to address the new market's audience and specific slant, of course. And you'll want to mention that this article was previously published in a noncompeting magazine (you might even include the clip). Otherwise, why argue with success? You know this letter works.

• *Send the clip of the published piece* to your target magazine's editor with a brief note that offers her reprint rights. This is a fine option when you're approaching markets that aren't likely to want revisions in the original article, such as newspaper travel sections or foreign magazines. Both can run straight pickups since almost none of their readers would have seen the original publication.

This won't be the best option if your original article's sources won't fit in at the new publication—if, for instance, all your sources for the church-member recruitment article were Presbyterians. Other denominations will look for at least a few sources drawn from their own ranks.

• *Circulate a menu of available articles.* List those articles you have in your "inventory," describe each in two or three sentences, and send it out with an SASE. This will be more effective if all the articles deal with a common theme (such as "church administration") and you target your mailing to magazines that routinely cover the topic.

Direct to manuscript

There are, of course, times when a query isn't appropriate or necessary. We'll look at those occasions in chapter nine.

Simultaneous queries

Sending identical queries to more than one market at a time is, to my mind, writing's biggest ethical gray area. I could easily defend a prohibition against the practice but for one fact: It takes too damn long to get an editor's response. If editors' responses came in, say, three or four weeks, that would not be an undue hardship on writers. But that's not the situation these days. Quoted response times extend up to two months, and reality may stretch that to three or four. (Among book publishers, the situation is even worse.)

So what's a writer to do? My best advice: Decide for yourself.

The worst-case scenario is that you'll have two competing editors asking for essentially the same article. As many writers have told me, "*That's* a problem? I should have such a problem!" But I've talked to writers in the midst of the worst-case scenario, and they never sound too excited about telling an editor, "I'm sorry, I can't take the assignment because I'm writing the article for your rival." It's not a statement designed to launch a beautiful friendship.

Yet I doubt the worst-case scenario is all that common. And the editor you must turn away may bear no ill feelings. I've only been turned away once for this reason—and the writer got the worst end because my magazine offered a higher payment. It is frustrating for the editor, but I *do* believe you'll clear the way by acknowledging in your query that yours is a simultaneous submission.

The final twist in this matter is that some magazines still object to simultaneous submissions—and say so in their guidelines and *Writer's Market* listings. My advice is to not send the query elsewhere simultaneously when submitting to these magazines. But I also recommend watching the response-time clock more closely. An editor who demands exclusivity also bears a responsibility to be prompt in her replies. If a response is overdue, send the editor a postcard notifying her that your submission is being submitted elsewhere. This still gives her the option to consider it but allows you to get on with your business.

If you choose to send queries out simultaneously, make sure your query follows the rest of the rules. Personalize the letter you send me, and slant it toward my audience. I remember receiving one query with a faint line between the "Dear Mr. Clark" salutation and the body of the letter; the writer had obviously photocopied the new address block onto a new letter. Better still, the typefaces didn't match!

The writer should have saved the stamp.

Multiple queries

This is an ethical escape hatch to the whole question of simultaneous queries: Propose multiple ideas related to a single overall topic. You're putting a half dozen queries into mail this way, but each query is for a different article and each is exclusive to a magazine. (Do not, however, send queries to competing magazines.)

For example, a trip to San Francisco might yield a half dozen travel articles, each focusing on a different aspect of the city for different markets. Or a writer proposing an informational piece on an old railroad station remodeled into a museum center (as was done in Cincinnati) might also seek out appropriate homes for a profile of the architect who led the renovation team, a roundup of several grand train stations converted to other uses, and a destination piece on the station's home city.

There's nothing dishonest about this practice, so long as each article is substantially different from the others. (That means a person who read more than one of the articles wouldn't think, "I've read this before.") In fact, working on three or four (or more) articles clustered around the same subject allows for more efficient researching and a better financial return on the time you invest in your reporting and writing. A final plus: Sending out a half dozen variations on an idea increases your chances of winning an assignment.

In-person queries

Depending on where you live, you may have opportunities to meet editors. In publishing's major cities, your next-door neighbor could be an editor. (Well, it could happen anywhere. But it's more likely in New York or Chicago.) It's also more likely you'll meet editors socially. But no matter where you live, attending a writers' conference will almost certainly allow you to come face to face with an editor.

In a social setting, an article pitch is just as rude as asking the doctor to diagnose your chronic back pain or soliciting tax advice from an accountant. It is acceptable to mention that you're a freelance writer; anything beyond that should only come in response to the editor's direct question. If you're familiar with the editor's publication, one useful tactic is to compliment a recent issue or specific article. This may lead to a general discussion about the editor's likes and dislikes and philosophies—all of which is invaluable information when you go home to brainstorm ideas and compose a query. Still at the party, if your comments impress the editor, she may ask about your writing and expertise. From there, who knows? Even if nothing more comes of it, you can at least remind her of the conversation when you decide to send a query.

At a writers' conference, the organizing committee may set up short one-on-one interviews between attending writers and participating editors. These are excellent opportunities to seek answers for particular questions raised in your study of the magazine's slant and editorial preferences, as well as general questions about how editors work. As for pitching specific ideas, different conferences have different rules of engagement. Ask the organizers for the ground rules when you register.

If you're allowed to pitch articles, don't expect to walk away from your interview with an assignment. Be prepared to briefly describe your topic and to answer questions, but also bring a query letter that explains the idea, a set of clips and an SASE. This gives the editor something to take back to the office for further consideration. (She may prefer you send the query to her office. In that case, include a note reminding her of your meeting and her interest, and mark the envelope "Requested Material.")

If the conference doesn't arrange these meetings, you can approach the editor yourself. Explain that you're interested in writing for her magazine and would appreciate a chance to talk over an idea or two. Give yourself a time limit and suggest a public meeting place. Your request might go something like this:

> Hi, my name is _____. I have a couple of ideas that I believe will work well in your magazine and was wondering if you might have a spare fifteen minutes to discuss them. The lounge seems pretty quiet; my treat?

If you're truly organized, you might send the query to the editor a couple weeks in advance and offer her the chance to further discuss the idea at the conference.

Treat any interaction with the editor as if it were a job interview. She will be sizing you up during this meeting, and you won't make a good impression by asking questions like, "So, what sort of magazine is *Writer's Digest*?" You never know where such meetings might lead; several years back, a writer introduced herself to me over the lunch table at a writers' conference. Throughout the meal, Susan asked intelligent questions about *Writer's Digest* and the types of articles we bought. Not too long afterward, I received a query that grew out of that conversation. Susan did such a good job with the assignment that when our Markets Editor position came open several months later, I called her. From that lunchtime conversation grew a monthly column that Susan wrote for about two years.

Queries by phone

Except in a couple of circumstances, *don't* reach for the telephone when you want to query an editor. First, you will interrupt the editor's day, so you risk her taking offense at the unscheduled break. Second, you're in a business that centers around words on paper. You won't dictate your article by phone, so why should you pitch your idea that way? If you have trouble understanding this taboo, ask yourself how highly you regard the telemarketers who call you at home to hawk portraits or aluminum siding. And this is how you want an editor to think of you?

There are two exceptions: If you have a long working relationship with an editor, she may invite you to call her with ideas. But you must wait for such an invitation; never presume it. (I, for one, never issue it.) The second exception is for an article that is urgently time sensitive. Say you've been banging on the door for an interview with a reclusive, major entertainment figure, and his handlers finally call. "Be here Tuesday," they say. Because you know you won't have a chance for follow-up questions after the interview, you might query the interview in a phone call to an appropriate editor. With her go-ahead in hand, you can be sure to ask questions appropriate to that audience. Such opportunities must be truly time sensitive, however, and involve an opportunity that just came up; this is not a procrastinating writer's salvation.

Queries by fax and electronic mail

Both fax and electronic mail operate over phone lines, so you shouldn't be surprised when I suggest you follow the same protocol I outlined for phone queries. However, these technologies allow a couple amendments to the standard of "Thou Shalt Not."

I think it's appropriate to fax or e-mail a note regarding an overdue response, especially for second and subsequent inquiries. And I would prefer a faxed or e-mailed query over a phone call regarding a time-sensitive topic (such as the one I described above). The fax or e-mail printout gives me something to look at and reread while I consider my answer.

I've never been good at fortune-telling, but I believe e-mail will eventually become an acceptable avenue for querying editors. There's already a fair amount of communication between editors and writers through the various on-line bulletin boards, and assignments are being made. I heard of one article that never hit paper until it was printed in the magazine; its query, assignment, writing, submission and editing were all done on computer and via modem. As more people are connected to computers, this form of communicating will become more common. And it does offer an immediacy that "snail mail" (as the Postal Service is known on-line) will never match.

Frequent contributor advantages

Several times in this chapter I've suggested that the rules are (or, more precisely, can be) different for regular contributors to a magazine. Just as merchants may give preferential treatment to customers they see every week, so editors allow the writers they work with regularly to take certain shortcuts. These shortcuts may be anything from waiving the need to send an SASE with each submission, to inviting phone queries, to adding the writer's name to the masthead as a "Contributor" or "Contributing Editor" or something similar.

Every editor handles such perks differently. But it is always the editor's choice. These are rewards to be passed out at the editor's discretion. Here's an example involving the salutation for a letter—a truly minor point, but one I pay attention to: I never address an editor by her first name until she's addressed a letter to "Dear Tom." (When I feel I've developed a professional friendship, I will sign my letters with just my first name as a friendly gesture, but that's as far as I'll push it.) It may strike you as a silly convention, but I find it off-putting when writers assume more of a relationship with me than they've earned. So I take care to avoid giving rise to those feelings in others. In freelancing, every advantage helps and every slight can hurt you. In the next chapter, we'll take a closer look at how editors react to your submissions.

CHAPTER EIGHT

On the Editor's Desk

Writers have taught me at least two facts: Editing is a mysterious profession, and editors are mysterious figures. Almost every time I speak to a group of writers—be it at a local club meeting or a large weekend conference—I can count on at least one person saying, "It's so good to meet an editor face to face. We only see the names in the magazine. It's nice to know that you're real people."

Such comments amuse me, not for their naiveté, but for the sense of celebrity these writers attach to editors and editing. I often wonder how they'd regard me if they saw me not as a name on the masthead, but as a husband who cleans off the supper table, or the father who can't seem to potty train his three-year-old, or the baseball fan who can't fathom why the manager hasn't pulled that pitcher yet. I am—as all editors are—just folks. A wordsmith by trade, but also spouse, parent, sibling, citizen, overworked, underpaid and overtaxed. You know, same as you.

I think it helps freelancers to remember that editors are, by and large, a fairly ordinary lot. We have a certain power over writers, sure. But it's no more power than you wield when you are choosing, say, which insurance agent will handle your business or which contractor you'll hire to build that addition onto your house. And just as you'll go with the agent who offers the best coverage or the contractor with the best plan for getting the job done on schedule, editors look for writers who can do the job right. And from the writer's side of the desk, that's power. But if your query letter suggests that you can give us editors what our magazines need, we'll gladly use whatever power we have to advance your career.

Beyond the mailbox

Once you mail your query letter, it will—God and the U.S. Postal Service willing—reach the intended editorial office. What happens then depends on several factors, the most important being the size of the magazine and its staff and the working style of the editor. We can draw a few generalities, though.

Your letter will land on the desk of the editor to whom it is addressed. That editor will at least thumb through her mail, pulling out those envelopes that bear the return addresses of her favorite writers (and writers whose assignments are overdue). The rest of the mail she'll pass along to an assistant; this person may handle every other editor's mail as well or (at larger magazines) work solely for your target editor. At some magazines, particularly smaller ones, the editor handles all the mail, reading and responding to everything. As I said, it all depends on size and inclination.

But let's say your target editor has passed your letter to her assistant. This staff member reads it and recognizes that your letter not only doesn't commit any major sins but proposes an idea that reflects an understanding of the magazine. This query, he decides, merits the editor's attention; it goes back to the editor's desk with a favorable report from the assistant. The editor reads the letter and either rejects it immediately or holds it for consideration.

What happens next depends on the magazine. The editor may be the sole decision maker, and she'll decide your query's fate right then. Or she might want another editor's opinion before making a decision and will pass your letter along with a request for comment. Or she might be a junior editor herself, which means she attaches her comments to your letter and sends it along to her peers for additional remarks or to her boss, who will render the final verdict.

At each step, your letter could be bounced back down the chain until it lands in your mailbox with a rejection note attached. And what you must know is that each time your letter is looked at, the reader/editor is looking for a reason to say "No."

Why I look to say "No"

Of all the unfairnesses! How can editors treat writers' work so callously as to *look* for reasons to say "No"? The answer is one of simple mathematics.

It's been years ago, but *Redbook* magazine's editors once estimated for a *Writer's Digest* survey that they received something on the order of thirty-six thousand manuscripts and queries each year. *Thirty-six thousand.* That figure boggles my mind, and it should make you gasp a bit, too. Relax—a little. Experience teaches editors that somewhere between half and three-quarters of all submissions are far enough off the mark to be rejected upon opening. The bigger the magazine, the more inappropriate submissions it attracts. So we'll reduce *Redbook*'s thirty-six thousand by the full three-quarters. That reduces your competition to a mere . . . (scribble, scribble, carry the three) . . . nine thousand submissions.

Hmmm.

Now let's open a recent copy of *Redbook* to its table of contents page. Counting everything, including those departments that could be staff written and therefore closed to freelance submissions, I find thirty-three articles in the magazine. For easy math's sake, we'll round it up to thirty-five. Times twelve issues a year, and we find that *Redbook* has slots for about 420 articles per year.

And nine thousand submissions from which to choose them.

I have a lot of trouble reading the *Racing Form*, and I can only remember winning money on a horse once. (A Derby winner named "Foolish Pleasure"; I liked the irony.) But even I recognize that 420-to-9,000 aren't great betting odds. It's better than the lottery, though, and look how many people play that every day. So don't rush out to have your head examined for still wanting to send that letter despite the odds. But you do need to be aware of what you're up against—and that's an editor who wants to say "No."

The editor wants to say "No" because she knows she must; she can't buy every idea that passes across her desk. Every editor learns early on that it's easier to say no at the query stage than it is after the manuscript is written or, worst of all, revised. It takes a couple times down the path, but eventually you learn. I even remember the name of the first writer who (unknowingly) taught me this lesson.

"It's a wonderful idea," I remember telling my editor.

"But the query isn't much," he said, pointing out what I didn't want to acknowledge.

"But I'm sure the article will be better. The writer just needs the right instructions."

"If you're willing to work with her . . . ," he said at last.

I *was* willing—two revisions worth. But my editor was right. The article never worked. And my final letter, the "I think we've gone as far as we can go with this, and it isn't far enough" letter, was twice as difficult to write because I knew I should have rejected the idea when I read the query. My inability to recognize the query's flaws to be fatal flaws cost everybody, especially the writer, a lot of work.

It's not my intention to make rejection sound somehow noble, as if editors are doing writers a favor by rejecting their queries. Even I don't have that much hubris. But every editor learns early on to harshly judge each letter she sees to avoid scenarios such as mine.

You, on the other hand, don't have to make it easy for the editor to say "no."

You start by heeding the advice that every editor gives: "Know Your Market." Know what sorts of subjects the magazine presents to its readers and what types of articles the editor favors. Then tailor your idea to fit in with these practices. I explained this study process in chapter two. If you skipped over it to get to the letter-writing stuff, go back. Absorb its lessons. This is critical information you'll need to even make the first cut.

Then write a compelling letter. Remember, your query letter is the best sample of your writing style that the editor has. Your clips may have been benefited from great editors, but your query is the unedited, unvarnished you. So the editor will study it for clues as to what sort of article she can expect from you.

In 1989, an editor named Keith Bellows spoke to a Society of Professional Journalists convention about query editors. As *Writer's Digest* Markets editor Chris Dodd reported in the magazine, Bellows described how he analyzes each query's structure to determine whether the writer is capable of handling an assignment. Bellows, who at the time of his remarks edited a series of very slick doctor's-waiting-room magazines called *Special Reports*, named six qualities he scrutinized. I've used his list below, adding my own comments on each.

• *The very first paragraph.* Does it grab the editor's attention, drawing her in and making her want to read more? The letter's opening is the topic of chapter four, but let me repeat the critical tip: Your letter's opening must be as seductive as your article's lead. If it's not, you may not have the editor's full attention when she reaches the heart of your idea.

• *Organization.* Is the letter well organized, spelling out logically how the writer plans to develop the story? If your 500-word letter rambles and skips and doubles back on itself and only talks about half the topic you promise to cover, the editor will be hard-pressed to think that you'll do better playing on a field that's four times the letter's length. Instead, she'll suspect that the article will be 2,000 words of meandering through only a portion of the topic.

• *Transitions.* This is also about organization, only on a micro-scopic level. Transitions are the words and phrases a writer uses to carry readers from one thought to the next without getting lost. The editor wants to see that you can process information smoothly, with-out jerking the reader from point to point.

• *Point of view.* What stance will you, the author, take on this topic? Viewpoint isn't the exclusive domain of essays and commentar-ies; in fact, it's the quality that separates magazine feature writers from just-the-facts newspaper reporters. And magazine editors want maga-zine writers.

• *Lively writing.* Does the query include the promise of color and detail that will bring this subject to life? If your query doesn't actually include anecdotes and quotes (as Sally-Jo Bowman's rain forest query did in chapter five), it must show that these essential elements will be in your article (as my in-laws query promised).

• *Length.* Does the writer wrap up the query quickly and effi-ciently? Bellows, like many editors, prefers one-page queries. If yours spills over to a second page, it had better have a good reason why. More than length, though, an editor will look to see if your query letter is a reflection of the article you're proposing. If you're promising a punchy, information-packed article or a gripping piece of drama, don't deliver that pledge in a windy, wordy, unfocused letter.

Fail on any of these quality checkpoints, and the editor will seize it as her opportunity to say "no." But handle these areas of concern well and editors will be suitably impressed; bear them in mind as you're drafting your letter. Also, look back to the section in chapter three on tone. This may look like a business letter you're composing, but it is actually the most important sample of your writing the editor has. Make it sparkle.

Other reasons for rejection

It is possible to write a perfectly fine query letter and still get back your SASE with a printed rejection. It's just like the car dealer who called you with a great new offer the day after you drove home a new car from another dealer. Or the investment opportunity that knocked at a time when your bank account stood at zero. Sometimes you'll be rejected for reasons other than the quality of your work. Here are seven such times:

Timing.

This is a line I've typed on many rejection letters: "You're idea is a good one. Unfortunately, it was a good one last week [or month, or year] when I assigned it to another writer." If you get this sort of response, celebrate your half-victory: It carries the triumph of having understood the market well enough to propose an appropriate idea. And such knowledge is empowering: Apply your market understanding to generate a new idea and submit it to the editor who responded to your first query. In this next letter, mention the near miss. Just get this one into the mail quickly; you want the editor to remember the earlier query. Within two or three weeks is best but certainly no longer than six weeks.

Sometimes it's hard for a newer writer to believe that another writer came up with "his" idea. This leads the writer to accuse the editor of stealing his idea and assigning it to someone else. I'll heed James Bond's advice and never say "never," but theft of ideas is as rare in the magazine industry as a soft-spoken host of a radio call-in show. Maybe it's rare because editors are fundamentally decent. (I said, "maybe". . . .) More likely, it's because theft doesn't make sense.

Editors do have their stables of favored writers. But these freelancers generally earned their way into the stable by proposing good ideas, fashioning them into publishable stories, and delivering them on time. Editors don't need to give one of these writers your idea; they're likely busy with their own ideas. Also, editors are eager to find new talent for their stables. Magazine writers have a nasty habit of burning out or dying or devoting themselves to writing books. The editor who's not constantly adding new writers will fairly soon wind up with an empty stable.

Idea theft makes no sense from an economic regard, either. The more articles you write for a market, the more you can expect to be paid for each assignment. So when you—an unfamiliar (to the editor) writer—come up with a strong idea, she can likely get away with paying you less than if she gave the job to one of her favored writers.

Charges of theft usually grow out of honest-to-goodness coincidences. Two (three, eight, twenty-seven) writers get basically the same idea at about the same time; the first compelling one to reach the top of the editor's in box wins. The rest see a similar article in print nine months later. One truth I've learned reading the mail is that if an idea is a good one, it'll show up again. And it won't take all that long.

"Not right for us."

The stereotypical rejection letter reads, "Thank you for your recent submission. Unfortunately, it does not meet our needs at this time." (My favorite variation on this was the one received by Snoopy in a "Peanuts" cartoon. The letter read, "You have not sent us anything in awhile. This meets our current needs.") The phrase "does not meet our needs" is a wonderful catchall expression that can mean anything from "You don't understand our market" to "I kinda like this and I kinda don't, so I'll be safe and say no." Just as an editor relies on gut instinct when she marks up a manuscript, so she does when judging queries. And there's not one thing a writer can do about it except live with it. But studying the market will give you the best chance of determining *how* to meet an editor's current needs.

"Not right for you."

A few times in my editing career I've allowed myself to hear my mother's admonition to always tell the truth and have flat out told writers that I was rejecting their work because it wasn't well written. I've done this maybe a half dozen times.

I have regretted each and every one.

In return for my lapse of judgment, I have heard my magazine insulted, my editorial judgment trashed, my own writing quality insulted, and my mother's marital status questioned. (Serves her right for filling my head with such silly admonitions.) I doubt I'll make the same mistakes again.

An editor may also feel you lack some needed skill other than pure writing ability. William J. Reynolds, who formerly served as managing editor at an in-flight magazine, once wrote in *Writer's Digest* that as an editor reading queries he would've liked to own a rubber stamp that read "Good Idea, But Not Right for You." Reynolds explained the need this way: "It's hard to read a good proposal from a good writer you know lacks the experience, sensitivity or finesse to bring the assignment off. And it's hard to tell a writer that. This is one of the reasons God invented 'Not right for us.' "

Office politics.

Whenever two or more people are gathered, egos get in the way. Assistant Editor Smith may be angling for a promotion over Assistant Editor Doe, and so runs down everything Doe pitches. Doe, of course, happens to be pitching your proposal to the Editor in Chief, who decides to let Smith have a minor victory before telling her that Doe got the job. Or the editor who likes your idea isn't being trusted right now because she also championed the cover story that bombed at the newsstand six months ago.

Budget.

Your idea may be excellent, but the editorial budget for manuscripts has run out. With luck, the editor will hold your query until the new fiscal year opens. Or she may ask you to try it again after a certain date. Then again, she may not.

Idiosyncrasies.

William Reynolds calls this "the quirk factor." I, for instance, really dislike titles that read "Confessions of . . ." or some replacement of the subject in "Everything You Ever Wanted to Know About _____, But Were Afraid to Ask." They're tired. And I'm tired of them. Use either, and your query must be a nudge better than someone else's to make me overlook your indiscretion. A more common quirk concerns those one-page query letters: I've heard a few editors say they won't look at two-pagers, and I've even heard one who said she wouldn't trust a letter that was *only* a single page.

You may never know if you've stepped on an editor's pet peeve. Your best defense is to learn everything you can about a market before you query. Hopefully, somewhere in the magazine's writer's guidelines, its *Writer's Market* listing, and whatever other reports you find on it, the editor will offer a clue about what not to write. Beyond that, simply do your best work.

It's a bad idea.

Realize that you will have them. Even the best hitters strike out occasionally. Luckily, an editor isn't likely to yell, "Yer out!" in front of fifty thousand people—or even tell you to your face. This is when "does not meet our current needs" is a kindness.

When your query is rejected

As much as we hope every idea finds a willing editor, the reality is that most of your ideas will be rejected. Salespeople of all types face the same syndrome: You hear "No" more often than you hear "Yes."

Too many writers look at a rejection as a catastrophic event. Don't. It's simply a part of freelancing. If you want to be a professional writer, you must steel yourself to read the word "No" a few times without going to pieces. I find that remembering three facts helps keep me sane:

Only your work has been rejected.

It's tempting to read a rejection as "Dear Writer: Your writing is without merit. You'll never be a writer. Quit now. Sincerely, All the Editors of the World." We invest a lot of ourselves in each idea we send out, so, naturally, when that pound of flesh is sent home unwanted, we reflect the rejection onto the rest of ourselves. But that is not what the editor meant. She meant just what the letter says, "This idea does not meet our needs at this time." This idea, at this moment, didn't work.

Your proposal has been rejected. You have not. Nor have you been crossed off the international list of acceptable writers. You're not even barred from sending a new idea to that same editor. There are no ramifications beyond the canceled stamps on your SASE.

In fact, sometimes the editor will make plain that her rejection is for this particular query only. The first query letter I sent to *Modern Bride* was wide of the magazine's editorial mark. In the rejection letter, the editor offered some advice for redirecting my idea generating and invited future submissions. Contrary to what you might suspect, such an invitation is *not* made out of courtesy. If an editor asks to see future ideas from you, she honestly wants to see future ideas. Editors receive quite enough mail; they don't need to invite more letters that will only require rejecting. The editor won't make a production of this (she's not courting Norman Mailer after all). But even a quick note—such as "This doesn't quite work for me, but please try again" scrawled across a form rejection letter—is an invitation you should take seriously. The door is open to you. I followed up my *Modern Bride* rejection with the in-laws query that I've quoted several times in this book. (In that query, I mentioned the previous correspondence and included a copy of the editor's note.) It sold, and so did the next.

It won't help to argue.

Instinct may tell you that you can talk the editor into changing her mind. Tell Instinct to go away. You may have been able to get your high school teachers to change that *D* to a *C* so Dad wouldn't ground you, but pleading won't work at this level. Arguing only brands you as an amateur. Accept the decision and try to figure out why it came. (But don't ask the editor to explain that, either. Her job is to choose articles for her magazine, not coach writers. She may decide to do that with a writer or two, but that is not an act she owes anyone.)

Put the idea back in the mail.

Just because you created this idea for a specific market doesn't mean it can't be reworked for someplace else. Perhaps in developing this idea you thought of other magazines where it might be appropriate. Now is the time to follow up on those thoughts and study those new options. If you have no such possibilities in mind, pull out your copy of *Writer's Market*. Scan the table of contents, noting which magazine categories might be appropriate for your idea. Then read through the listings in those categories in search of new publications to research and, perhaps, submit your story to.

The rules don't change when you send a rejected query to a new market. You still must study the magazine, you still must focus your idea for the readership, you still must craft a letter that connects your idea to that audience. All this means more work before you put the idea back into the mail. But an idea can't sell if it's sitting in your desk drawer. You must keep your work circulating.

When the answer isn't "No"

While into every writing life a little rejection must fall, that's not the outcome you're hoping for. You want the encouraging word. But what can you expect when it comes?

A positive response will most often come in one of four fashions. I'll call the first a "holding pattern": For whatever reason, the editor is unable to make a decision at this moment. (Perhaps, as I suggested earlier, the editorial budget is temporarily dry.) So she asks you for permission to hold onto your letter. Your response depends on one factor: Can you wait? If you believe the idea will sell more quickly at another magazine, you might choose to not wait. Pay rates and timeliness and market prestige enter into this decision, as well. But if the editor asking to hold your query is one you'd like to break in with, agreeing to wait can help establish you as a writer she appreciates.

If you decide to not grant her request, don't worry about being blacklisted at that publication. It's your idea, and you have a right to decide its fate. And any editor who refuses to concede that point shouldn't be an editor you want to work with. If you do allow her to hold the idea, ask her when you can expect a decision. If that date passes without word, withdraw the query and send the idea elsewhere.

The second type of positive response is a request to learn more. I've asked writers for more information when a query has whetted my interest but failed to fully outline the article. Other times I've needed to know about some aspect of the subject. Perhaps the writer has offered to "share several good techniques" for achieving some purpose; I may ask for four or five of them to decide if my audience will really find them useful. (I remember one query in which the query's topic escaped our editorial staff. As I remember it, our response was along the lines of, "Sounds interesting. But what is it?" The author answered our question and, eventually, sold the article.)

Respond to this request as quickly as possible, providing enough information to satisfy the editor's questions. Now is not the time to skimp. The editor has opened the door for you, but you'll need to fully answer her questions. Frankly, if I don't get everything I need in reply, I don't ask again. If a writer won't—or can't—respond to a need this simple, I write him off as a problem I don't need.

A third positive response is an "on-spec" assignment ("spec" is short for "speculation"). Some editors use this as a risk-free tool for dealing with writers they've not worked with before. It's a qualified "yes," a request to see the article but one without the promise of purchase that is understood in a full assignment. Nor will a kill fee be paid if the article is rejected. In essence, an editor who makes an on-spec assignment is saying, "I'm interested in your idea—very interested, in fact. But I'm leery because we haven't worked together previously. So here's the deal: You write the article, and I'll read it. If I like it, I'll buy it. If I don't, I won't. Fair enough?"

Now it's your call. Professional writers, understandably, object to on-spec work. The editor is asking the writer to put forth substantial effort with no promise of a payoff at the other end. But unless you have a long list of publication credits that you didn't mention in your query, you probably can't convince the editor to upgrade an on-spec offer to a full assignment.

Beginning writers probably need to consider on-spec work part of the dues they must pay to establish themselves. Some editors will *only* work on spec with writers new to them. If you want to crack such markets, you may have no choice. It is, after all, an opportunity to sell an article; you have the editor's agreement to at least consider your work. Yours will be a solicited submission. And that's more than you had last month.

You can improve your article's chance of acceptance by making sure you understand what the editor wants to see. (I'll discuss this further in a moment.) And definitely follow up with a short note accepting the on-spec assignment. If the editor didn't set a deadline, tell her when you expect to deliver the article. And, of course, thank her for the opportunity. Then write the best article you can.

The final positive response you can expect from an editor is both the most common and the best: an assignment. This is just like what you used to get in school, except this isn't five hundred words that will determine whether you get an *A* or a *B* for the quarter. We're talking cash now.

In her assignment letter, your editor should furnish the following information:

A deadline.

This can be anywhere from a couple weeks to a few months. Unless otherwise noted, consider it chiseled in stone. If you can't meet it, let the editor know as soon as possible—certainly sooner than the day before she expects it in the office. Some editors schedule articles to run quite soon after their deadlines; even a week's delay in receiving the piece can throw off the careful choreography each piece must follow on its way into the magazine.

A length.

This is nearly always expressed in numbers of words. (And yes, when you're counting words, you must count them all—even the teeny ones like *a*, *I* and *the*.) A manuscript that comes within 10 percent of the assigned word length is generally acceptable. For instance, a writer assigned a 2,000-word article will be safe if the word count falls between 1,800 and 2,200. *Do not* expect your editor to do your dirty work when it comes to cutting; no editor on earth appreciates the manuscript cover letter that reads, "I know you only wanted 1,500 words, but I found the topic so fascinating that I wrote 5,000. Consider using them all—your readers will love it. But if you can't, I'll rely on your good judgment." That's damning with feint praise, and the writer is the person being damned.

A payment.

The editor's letter should clearly set down the fee you'll receive for completing the assignment. It should also say when you will receive this payment—on acceptance or on publication. "On acceptance" means that the check-writing process begins when you complete the assignment (including any needed rewrites) and the editor says the piece is ready for publication. "On publication" means the check-writing process doesn't begin until your article waits for its slot in an issue, is edited, laid out, printed and sent to subscribers. That process can be a matter of days, in the case of a newspaper, or a matter of months— even years—at some magazines. Guess which type of payment most writers favor?

Wouldn't you know, the smaller magazines that tend to be more open to newer writers are also more likely to pay on publication. So it's new writers who most frequently wind up with no money to show for their "sold" articles. And may never see their payments, since smaller magazines are more likely to sink in a sea of red ink. There are strategies for negotiating better deals (I hesitate to call them "fairer" deals because I don't believe anything less than pays on acceptance is fair; try telling the folks at Circuit City that you'll send a check for the washing machine *after* you run through the first load). Freelancer Gregg Levoy offers several in his book *This Business of Writing* (Writer's Digest Books).

A kill fee.

Sometimes an assignment just doesn't work out. Either the writer wasn't capable of putting together an article that satisfied the editor, or the topic fell apart once the digging started. Regardless, the article isn't publishable, and the assignment must be "killed." Rather than being obligated for the full price in such cases, magazines often insert a contract provision that allows for a reduced payment, which is called a kill fee. Generally, the kill fee is between 10 and 25 percent of the full assignment fee, although payments of a third to one-half aren't unheard of.

One all-too-common reason for canceling an assignment is a change at the publication, either a new editor or a turn in editorial directions. (Usually, the latter results from the former.) This turn of events shouldn't trigger a kill fee since the writer had no role in the article becoming unpublishable. Writers' advocates argue that in such cases the publisher is obligated for the full fee. But publishers in transition have been known to cancel assignments, pay the kill fees, and hope the writers take the money and go away. If you learn of a major change at a publication while you're working on an assignment, immediately call to make sure your piece is still wanted.

A rights-purchased statement.

Gregg Levoy's book can also help you get a grasp on what you must know about this complex and sometimes confusing issue of copyright. This knowledge won't improve your writing or even your chances of winning an assignment, but it will help you retain control over what you write and sell. For our purposes, it's enough for you to know that when an editor "buys" your article, she is actually leasing your copyright in the piece. (It's about the same as renting an apartment from a building's owner; you don't get to keep the apartment forever, just for the length of time specified in your lease.) The rights statement in the editor's acceptance letter tells you how the magazine would like the terms of that lease to read.

It is in your best interest to sell only "first rights"; that means you agree to let the magazine be the first publisher of the work. In the United States and Canada, the most common rights arrangement is "first North American serial rights." In such arrangements, the writer licenses the publication to be the first magazine in North America to print the article. (The word "serial" in this phrase refers to the magazine being a serial publication; it doesn't mean your article will be broken up and run over several issues.)

If you do not understand what rights your editor wants to buy, ask her to explain it. Keep asking until you do understand it. Otherwise, *you* could wind up having to ask *the magazine* for permission to reprint your own article. (This occurs when you sell "all rights.") The Copyright Office at the Library of Congress, (202) 479-0700, can also provide answers to your questions.

Notes on writing the article.

Very often an editor will offer her comments on what she would like to see in your finished article. It might be an emphasis on a particular part of the topic or a warning about an area that's tripped up previous writers on the topic or a piece of your outline she doesn't want in the article. Heeding such remarks will help you write an acceptable article the first time around.

If your editor's acceptance letter doesn't include any piece of this information, call her and ask the questions directly: "Did you have any suggestions concerning the article? Does the query's outline cover the topic all right? Your assignment is for first rights only, correct?"

It is possible that your editor will make the assignment in a phone call. Make detailed notes of the editor's comments, especially regarding the content of the article. If you forget some point and need to call her back, she may be no more likely to remember what she said. The editor may follow up your conversation by sending you a contract that states such particulars as purchase price, rights and deadline. If not, draft a quick note that notes the terms you agreed to over the phone. Send the note to your editor with a request to "let me know if I misunderstood any of the terms."

It's vital to have the terms of your assignment in writing. Misunderstandings occur. At those times, it's critical to have a piece of paper that you can point to and say, "This is what you told me, and you didn't correct me when I sent you a copy." Every writer hopes to avoid such occasions, but it's better to be ready for them.

Before you agree to an assignment, consider what's being offered. Is the fee fair, or at least in line with the pay rates mentioned in the magazine's *Writer's Market* listing? Are you happy with the rights arrangements? Can you meet the deadline? Many writers don't believe that negotiation is possible. But it is. (Whether it's successful is another matter.) I heard of one writer who routinely asks for double the price offered by the editor. While he rarely gets that much, the request for more almost always brings an increase over the first offer.

If negotiations prove fruitless and you remain unhappy with the terms you're offered, you do have the option to walk away. Of course, the editor has the option to let you go, and you will lose the sale. In the longer view, you'll feel better for standing by what you believe is fair compensation. I remember actually being impressed by one writer who had queried *Writer's Digest* but who turned down my assignment. "I'm sorry," he said after trying unsuccessfully to negotiate a particular payment. "I told myself a couple years ago that I wouldn't accept less than twenty-five cents a word anymore. I'd really like to write this piece for you, but it's not the best thing for me to do."

Depending on your haggling skills, you may not feel comfortable asking for more money. But as you gain experience, you should see your pay rise. Especially when you're getting third and fourth assignments from an editor. Once you've proven you can write for a market, the editor should be willing to increase your pay. But you will almost always have to ask her for it.

Response times

"I mailed my query six weeks ago and haven't heard a word. How long should I wait?"

That has to be the most frequently asked question among writers who call *Writer's Digest* for advice. In most cases, a magazine's listing in *Writer's Market* will tell you what the editor's average response time is. On occasion, the editor will note separate response times for queries and for manuscripts. Most fall between three weeks and two months; whatever is listed, expect it to be longer during the summer and over the Christmas holidays when vacations typically disrupt the normal office routine.

My general rule for both queries and manuscripts is to allow an editor two weeks more than the response time she reports in *Writer's Market*. Then I follow up with a brief note that says something like this:

> On [date], I mailed you a query for an article I called "[title]." Since I haven't received your response, I was afraid that either my letter or yours went astray. So I've enclosed another copy of my query. I look forward to hearing from you at your earliest convenience.

If your overdue submission was an article, simply rephrase the note accordingly. Resubmitting the article is a matter of choice, but if the piece is short, I'd send it.

As an editor, I like this approach. I know that the letter most likely went astray in my in box, and I'm pretty sure the writer knows it, too. But he casts no aspersions and, thus, I take no offense. And enclosing a copy of the missing query means I don't have to go diving in my in box—a task I might not have time for right then (even if I were brave enough to do it). I can read the letter and make my decision immediately.

With this note, I'd also enclose at least one clip (even if you sent them with the first letter; remember, it's missing in action) and, definitely, an SASE. This is also an excellent opportunity to update the editor, as in: "Since I queried you, I completed an assignment for [magazine]." Or you might pass along some bit of information that you'll use in the article you proposed. Treat this note as another chance to sell the editor on you and your idea.

If the follow-up note brings no response in the next two to three weeks, you are justified in phoning the editor. Call the editorial office (the number should be in your sample issues, or call Information), and ask for the editor you addressed your envelope to. Resist the urge to sound indignant or accusatory. Simply explain that you submitted a query/manuscript on this date and a follow-up on that date, and you haven't received a response. Ask if a decision has been made and, if not, when you might expect an answer. If the editor is unsure, ask if it would be helpful for you to send another copy of your work. (Being helpful really raises the editor's guilt quotient; I'd sooner dive into my in box than feel guilty.)

When you phone, you may only get to the editor's assistant. That's OK, but his response will likely be along the lines of "I'll have to check with the editor." Say you understand, and then ask when it would be convenient for you to call back for an answer. This is more far more effective than leaving your number and waiting for the assistant to call you back with the information.

Don't expect to get the editor's "yes" or "no" over the phone; your goal is just to kick loose a response. But if another two weeks pass without something in the mailbox, it's time to cut bait and try other waters. Send the editor another note, outlining the history of your submission and follow-ups. Then add: "I hope to work with you in the future, but I am withdrawing my query/manuscript to submit it elsewhere."

The important note to strike in all this correspondence is neutral professionalism. Accusations *never* help; they only cause the editor to raise her defenses. And, who knows, maybe extraordinary circumstances have led to the delay. Your job is to sell your idea. And if not this one, then the next. Give the editor the benefit of the doubt, but protect yourself. Once the response is overdue, start revising the idea for submission at another market. Take your revenge by selling the article elsewhere (at a competing magazine makes the revenge *really* sweet).

CHAPTER NINE

From Queries to Articles

After the query, after the research, and after the writing and revising and writing, you hold a finished article. From here on, the rules are largely dictated by common sense. Still, there are areas to proceed through cautiously to avoid the missteps that will instantly mark you as an amateur.

As with your query letters, your goal in preparing and submitting manuscripts is to appear as professional as possible. This doesn't require an office full of high-tech equipment. But attention to the details I'll discuss in this chapter will keep editors coming back to you with new and more challenging assignments.

When a query isn't necessary

There are a (very) few magazines whose editors actually prefer to see a complete manuscript. And another group of editors who say they'll look at either queries or manuscripts. These preferences will be stated in *Writer's Market* or in the magazines' writer's guidelines. Given the choice, I'd still choose to send a query, if for no other reason than the letter allows me the luxury of judging the marketplace before I research and write and rewrite. Throw in the opportunity to hear the editor's thoughts on what to include in the article, and I see the query as the clear winner.

So, in most situations, a query letter is the most appropriate way to contact an editor when you want to write for a magazine. But even at publications where the editors have a "query first" policy, a manuscript sent in "over the transom" (that is, unsolicited) will likely get read—and perhaps bought. But unsolicited manuscripts receive the lowest priority, making a sometimes interminable wait even longer. And rightfully so. You've ignored the published wishes of the editor by choosing to bypass the query stage and send the manuscript.

However . . .

There are a few specific types of articles that simply don't hold up when they're reduced to a few paragraphs in a query letter. In these cases, most editors prefer to see a complete manuscript.

- *The Essay.* These articles are often built around a specific situation, but they take their power from the writer's ability to connect a commonplace event or thought to an insight with universal impact. Reduced to a paragraph or two, an essay may sound pompous or downright silly. And even if you could offer a compelling abstract, that talent doesn't allow an editor to judge your ability to carry the theme over a whole piece or to believe in the writing's quality. And those two aspects of an essay are key to its success.

- *Humor.* Most of the best humor pieces are essays that approach their topics lightly or wryly. Or they take the Dave Barry approach and exaggerate their situations to tremendous proportions. Neither lends itself to effective previewing. In fact, my internal alarms begin clanging whenever I read in a cover letter, "The enclosed is my humorous look at . . ." If you feel obligated to tell me the article is supposed to bring a smile to my face, we're both in trouble.

- *Fillers.* A filler is a very short piece, usually three or four paragraphs long, but sometimes only a few lines in length. The classic example is the *Reader's Digest* anecdote, but many other magazines look for humorous fillers as well. A punch line isn't always desired, however. In some magazines, fillers are simply brief news reports or nuggets of information.

- *Very Short Department Articles.* Magazines that use such pieces often collect them under a department headline such as Almanac or Briefings or (as in *Writer's Digest*) Tip Sheet. These departments often appear in the opening third of their magazines, but not exclusively.

The articles that run in them may, like fillers, be humorous anecdotes or tips or news briefs. Or they may be somewhat more substantial—running up to 500 words. Only studying sample issues and a market's writer's guidelines will reveal what departments a magazine has and what length article is appropriate for these departments. But to query these items would require writing a letter containing more words than the item. That's a good rule of thumb: If your query would require more words than the article it pitches, skip the letter.

Of course, there are some editors who *will* want to see a query for one or another of these article types. As always, check the magazine's *Writer's Market* listing and read its writer's guidelines before you drop anything in the mail. If the editor lists no exception to her "query first" policy, then you must find a way to write a compelling letter.

As with any other query, your goal will be to isolate the central idea of the article you propose. That should actually be quite easy in a shorter piece, where there may only be room for one idea, and in an essay, which is built around its theme. Querying a humor piece will require you to play up the article's hook: the twist on a subject of interest to the magazine's readers. But you'll need to do more than simply label the article "humorous"; incorporate your light touch and exaggerations into your outline of the article.

Don't be afraid of being brief in this query; it doesn't make any sense to write 500 words to query a 300-word manuscript. In the most straightforward language possible, preview the article's contents and benefits. A short article should require no more than a paragraph. If you can't meet that standard, you better ask whether your idea is too large.

Cover letters

Before we look at what a cover letter is, I want to tell you what it often isn't: necessary. In many cases—particularly when you decide to ignore the editor's wishes (and my advice) and send an unsolicited manuscript—you don't need to send a cover letter. Simply address the envelope to the appropriate editor, format the first page of the manuscript as I'll show you in a minute, and send it (with SASE, of course).

The only time to send a cover letter is when you have information the editor must know. Such information might be: that you spoke with the editor about the piece, that you've met the editor (at a writers' conference, for instance), that you have significant personal experience with the topic of the article, that the article previously appeared elsewhere, that someone the editor knows and—you hope—respects suggested you send the piece to her, or that you have very impressive publication credits.

Cover letters don't need to be long—in fact, editors appreciate brevity in the form. Yet many writers feel the need to ramble on as if they're composing the year-end review letter to fold into everybody's Christmas card.

Not too long ago *Writer's Digest* received a memorable poetry submission. One poem with a cover letter. The poem was twelve lines long; the letter, nineteen. The writer began by describing the particular writing experience that inspired the poem. That took five lines. In the next paragraph, he used three sentences to say his poem was enclosed and that he felt it was "suitable for *Writer's Digest*." (I guess that's why he sent it to us!) He gave the poem's title, and its subject, and its length. In the third paragraph, he used five more sentences to tell us that through *Writer's Digest*, he'd gotten an idea that led to about two dozen articles appearing in his local newspaper, found a little poetry journal that had published his first poem, learned about a poetry contest in which he was now a finalist, and started searching for a publisher for his recently completed genre novel. Finally:

> I hope you agree that [the poem's title] would be a good humorous poem to be published in *Writer's Digest*. If you have any questions, call me at [phone number]. Thank you for your time, and I hope to hear from you soon.

Oh, he heard. He heard that his poem didn't fit our current needs. But it may be years before this writer figures out that his cover letter painted him an amateur before his poem ever got a chance to be judged objectively.

Compare that letter to this one, which arrived on an unsolicited article. This article was rejected, too, but not because the writer scared off the editors before they reached page one.

Enclosed is an article for your consideration.

I am a retired librarian whose poems have been published in *The Mickle Street Review, Arete: The Journal of Sport Literature, The Haight Asbury Literary Review, Exit 13, Fan: A Baseball Magazine* and other magazines. I am the author of three books of poetry, *Cliff Walk* and *Silhouettes at Eventide*, self-published under my own imprint of Moveable Feast Press, and *Chinese Camp and Other California Poems*, published by Sunstone Press of Santa Fe, New Mexico.

Thank you for considering my article for publication in *Writer's Digest*.

This letter may not be perfect (personally, I'd leave out the notation that the writer is retired; prejudices abound, and why offer yourself up as a victim?), but it's short, direct and informative. I don't learn the creative history of the submission or the writer's rationale for sending it to me—and I thank the writer for that courtesy.

I also would not have felt the loss if this writer had skipped sending the letter. His publishing history, while not skimpy, also isn't likely to knock the socks off the editors of a national publication. The information would have made the same impact if the writer had placed it in a bionote following the end of the article.

Of course, there are some writers who simply must put a cover letter on everything they send out. If your DNA is so wired, then draft letters that give a sense of your style, that will stand out from the flock of letters beginning, "Please find enclosed . . ." *GQ* editor Martin Beiser showed *WD* freelancer Judy Mandell "the best letter I ever received." It read:

Dear Mr. Beiser,

Let me put it this way: It's unsolicited, it's funny, and it's enclosed.

Sincerely,

"When it's that authoritative," added Beiser, "you can't not read the piece. And [the author] was right. It was very funny." And, shortly thereafter, it was very published.

I admit it, a compelling cover letter *can* intrigue an editor. But it's a risk. Beiser's correspondent was cocky enough to write a letter that didn't do anything more than say, "Here it is." Not every writer has such self-confidence—and not every article will be served by the one-line approach. But if you feel you must introduce your manuscript with a letter, strive to be creative and keep it short.

Limiting yourself to a short letter also increases the likelihood that your letter will be read. Frequently, that cover letter you labored over is only going to be skimmed (which further demonstrates why cover letters aren't usually necessary). The editor pulls the submission from the envelope, glances over the letter in search of something noteworthy—such as an impressive credit or a familiar name—and then turns directly to the submission. A long, rambling letter like the poet's above attracts the eye, too, but not in the manner a writer wants. In fact, Writer's Digest Books editor Jack Heffron wrote in *Writer's Digest* that cover letters are more useful *after* a submission has been read. It's after the manuscript has been reviewed and liked that the editor will want to learn about the author.

Before you feed that piece of letterhead into the printer, ask yourself if this letter is really necessary. When in doubt, let your work introduce itself.

One time to definitely include a cover letter is with any article that has been invited by the editor. This is particularly true of on-spec assignments, which—because of their uncertain, speculative nature—may not be considered in her issue-by-issue planning, or even be remembered by the editor. Your cover letter exists to remind her that she asked to see this piece (although you needn't phrase it so bluntly). For pieces submitted on spec, you might even include in your package a photocopy of the editor's invitation. (I hate to think the worst of people, but I remember receiving two or three articles labeled "on spec" that I'm sure I never invited. A copy of my invitation—if one existed—would have removed the mystery.)

Beyond prodding your editor's memory, your letter might note anything unusual about the piece or some matter the editor should know before editing it. When appropriate, a comment regarding available artwork can be helpful. And if you will be out of contact for a period of time during the next month or so—say, you're vacationing or tied up on other projects—tell her the dates when you can't be reached.

Finally, you'll earn a brownie point or two by expressing your willingness to revise the article as needed and thanking her for the opportunity.

Here's the cover letter that accompanied an assigned manuscript from writer John Calderazzo. (Despite his apologies, the article was only slightly behind its time.) Notice how Calderazzo prepared me for an article that was a departure from the traditional *Writer's Digest* how-to article.

> Dear Tom,
>
> Finally, dammit. Sorry it took so long.
>
> I'll skip the usual excuses and just say I got caught up in this much more than I thought I would. I've really tried hard to get down something distinctive that also offers—based on lots of my teaching—practical advice based on what I think young or beginning essay writers genuinely need to know. (For instance, the small lists of writers and periodicals in step 16—even some of my most talented graduate students don't know where to look for the best stuff.) My overall approach is impressionistic, and some of it may seem strange (though it isn't to me and probably won't seem so to most personal-essay writers), but this is also the most pragmatic approach I can think of. Really.
>
> So, I hope you like the thing. This is about the best writing I know how to do.
>
> Many many thanks for your understanding patience. I'll be waiting for your response.

Like Martin Beiser after reading the one-line cover letter, I couldn't wait to read this manuscript. And, amazingly, Calderazzo hadn't oversold the article. He also showed me a writer who cares about doing work that is challenging and creative even as it remembers its obligation to the audience.

Calderazzo's letter also reminds us that a writer's letters to editors aren't business correspondence. There's no mistaking that this letter is the work of a creative writer, and I think it's one-to-one conversational tone strikes the proper chord. (Although I don't recommend making a habit of using "dammit" in your first sentence.) It's informal, but professional—a reflection of Calderazzo's relationship with me and *WD*. For the record, the article was his second assignment.

Manuscript mechanics

For whatever reason, a lot of mystery surrounds the technical subject of formatting a manuscript. As with the physical appearance of your query letter, you want your manuscript to look as if a professional sent it. The shocking truth about manuscript mechanics is this: It ain't that big a deal. Beyond a few rather obvious specifications, the best guide you can have is old-fashioned common sense.

Since you are, by now, thinking like an editor, you will want to make your manuscript easy on the eyes. To that end, you will begin with white paper. As it was for your query letter, a ream (paper talk for packs of five hundred sheets) of the stuff used in photocopiers will be just fine. A 20-pound bond is even nicer. Anything heavier is overkill. And erasable bond remains a no-no.

On this pristine white paper, you will print or type firm, dark black letters. No faded ribbons, no half-dead toner cartridges. If you're still hanging on to that typewriter, the original keys or type ball will produce acceptable type. If your printer offers dozens of options, pick a boring, serif typeface and set the machine for twelve points. If you're attacked by an urge to liven up your manuscript with other fonts or special effects, shoot it. The last thing a professional wants his manuscript to be is cute.

Again, text produced on near letter-quality dot matrix printers is generally acceptable, although I still hear a few disagreeable souls claim to reject dot matrix out of hand. Yet there is no denying that manuscripts printed on a laser or ink-jet printer are easier to read and, therefore, look more professional.

Double-space your lines of text, which means leave a line of space between each line of text. This makes the manuscript easier for the editor to read. It also allows her to mark insertions between the lines when editing. Margins are an editor's other writing space; leave white space of between one inch and one and one-half inches all around. If your letters are printed in a type smaller than 12-point, go for the larger margin. You want an open-looking page, which is more inviting to the eye.

Some word processing programs allow you to justify your text—that is, to add space equally between the words on a line so each line runs from the left margin all the way over to the right margin. (Just as the text appears here; book text is justified.) Do *not* access this feature. Justified text looks fine in published columns on a book or magazine page but is tiring to read when stretched across a manuscript page. Leave the right margin ragged.

Don't worry too much about page breaks within a paragraph. This isn't your high school English class. No editor concerns herself with that level of minutiae; if she does, she needs better articles to read. If a new page's first line has just one or two words on it, you might fiddle with the paragraph to keep those few words on the preceding page. Or if a page's last line is a subhead, you might want to force the page break prior to the subhead. But don't lose sleep over such matters.

If you want a line of white space to appear at some point in your printed article, you must note it in your manuscript. On an otherwise blank line, center a series of three or four asterisks (*) or pound signs (#) or the words "line space" within brackets. Writers often use these breaks to indicate a major time or place transition or to mark the start of a new section.

If your manuscript uses an extended quote from a printed source—a several-line excerpt from a letter, diary or book, perhaps—you should indicate that this material is to be set off from the rest of the manuscript. You can do this by reducing the left and right margins adjacent to the excerpt (maintain the double spacing between the lines, though) or note in brackets the start and finish of the section, as in "[Begin block quote]" and "[End block quote]."

Other special circumstances may come up as you type a specific manuscript. And while these issues may seem terribly important, they usually aren't. If you must track down an answer, consult *The Associated Press Stylebook and Libel Manual* (Addison-Wesley) for text questions and *The Chicago Manual of Style* (University of Chicago Press) for manuscript styling concerns. Most often, though, you can apply common sense: Ask yourself how to put this point on the page in a way that is easy to read while communicating what you need done. And then use that way consistently through the rest of the manuscript.

Page one setup

The first page of your manuscript has the important task of telling readers who submitted this manuscript. This information should appear on the first page even if you send a cover letter (which, I repeat, may not be necessary) or attach a title page (which is never necessary for an article). Your cover letter may be routed elsewhere in the office, and your title page will most likely be torn off. But you can feel certain that your page one will remain with its fellow pages.

In the top left-hand corner of your first page goes the address block. In this block will be your name, street address, city, state and zip code, and daytime phone number. Position that information in four or more single-spaced lines. If you generally use a post office box, consider listing a street address under it; express delivery services such as FedEx and Overnight Mail can't deliver packages to post office boxes, and overnight letters are increasingly common.

That's the required information: name, address and phone number. There's other data that can be included at the top of your manuscript, but it's all optional.

Many writers also list their Social Security numbers immediately under their phone numbers. To conform with current tax laws, a publisher can't issue payment without this number, and many writers believe adding their number to the manuscript speeds up payment. Possibly. I don't list mine, however; I don't want a publisher to issue me a check without first discussing the price with me. It's your choice.

Over on the right-hand side of the page is space for more data. On the top line, list your manuscript's word count. An exact count isn't necessary; round off the number to the nearest hundred. (Round it off to the nearest fifty for pieces of fewer than 1,000 words; the nearest ten for fillers of fewer than 100 words). "About 1,500 words" works well for a 1,353-word manuscript.

Under the word count, you can skip a line and state the rights you're offering for this article. Again, this is optional and not something I ordinarily do. The magazine has a rights arrangement it normally requests (typically first North American serial, as we discussed in chapter seven), and the editor will make that request regardless of what you list on this line. One exception: If you're offering reprint rights to a previously published piece, type in

"Reprint rights offered" just to make this clear.

Some writers replace the rights-offered line with a formal copyright line, as in "Copyright © 1995 by Thomas Clark." (This line is also commonly placed at the manuscript's end.) I see nothing particularly wrong with this practice; in fact, some commentators suggest the Copyright Act encourages the placement of this line on every document. But you should know it offends some editors. These editors argue—however irrationally—that typing this line on your manuscript suggests you share the amateur's fear that editors steal submitted articles. These editors consider the notice an insult to their integrity. By that logic, of course, I should believe my neighbor stenciled his name on his mailbox because he was afraid I'd steal his house. Sorry, comrades, this one doesn't wash.

And yet . . . since I know there are editors who will think poorly of me for including a copyright notice, I leave it off. This may be the moral equivalent of writing TV sitcoms for the dimmest viewer, I suppose, but I'll take the risk.

After you arrange the address block and put down whatever optional data you choose to, drop down several lines until you're between one-third and halfway down the page. On this line, center your article's title. You can type it in all capital letters or in upper- and lowercase letters with quote marks on both ends. If your article is intended for a specific department or column, type its name before your article's title.

Tip Sheet: "Page One Setup"

Skip a line and type your byline as you wish it to appear in the magazine.

"Queries and Submissions"
by Thomas Clark

Blame it on Samuel Clemens, but many writers entertain the notion of writing under a pseudonym. Maybe they're writing exposés of their employers or a trashy confession story to make a buck while they work on the Great American Novel; whatever the reason, they're anxious to keep their real names off of this story. If you plan to use a pseudonym, type that name below your article's title. But use your real name in the address block at the top of the page. That's the name the publisher will type on the check. (If you don't want the publisher to know your real name, then you'll need to arrange a "doing business as" card at the bank where you'll deposit your checks.)

Now, double-space again, and start typing your article.

The last line of every page—except the last page— should only bear the word "More." It may be centered or run flush with the right-hand margin. This tells the editor that more text is found on the next page.

Following pages setup

Pages two through the end of your article should include what's called a "slugline." The elements of a slugline are your last name, a key word or phrase from your article's title and the page number. Separate the elements with commas or dashes or slashes, and type it flush left on the top line of the page:

Clark/Queries—2

The slugline—or "running head," as it's also called—lets the editor reassemble the manuscript quickly when she drops it. Your name and title are on the line in case your manuscript gets dropped along with someone else's.

And you thought publishing was so technical, huh?

Following the slugline, double-space and pick up the text of the article from the previous page. Whether you're typing your manuscript or trusting a computer to print it out, double-check the continuity of the text from the end of one page to the beginning of the next.

The rest of the text in your article should be presented as straightforwardly as possible. If you want to indicate that a book title or other word is to run in italic type, simply underline it. It's not necessary (or wanted) to change the printer font to actually show the word in italic. The editor will need to underline it before sending the manuscript to the typesetter, anyway. If you wish a word or phrase to appear in boldface type, mark a squiggly line underneath it.

Many magazines use subheads within an article. These short headlines (generally between two and six words) visually break up solid blocks of text on a page, but they can also help writers organize the flow of information and help readers search out a particular section when they need to. For instance, if you were in the midst of typing a manuscript and needed to locate my tips on sluglines, you'd skim this chapter for the "Following Pages Setup" subhead above.

If your target publication uses subheads, you can stage a subtle demonstration of your familiarity with the market by including them in your manuscript. Study the magazine to see where the subheads are placed in the text—and what style is preferred. Some editors prefer straightforward label subheads (the type I've tended toward in this book), others lift specific phrases from the text, and some prefer gags, puns, or the whole range of word play.

As you write additional pages, continue the pattern of typing "More" and sluglines until you reach the article's end. After the final line of text, double-space and type "The End" in the center of the line. Sometimes the notation is "—30—", which is an old newspaper symbol.

After typing "The End," you can drop down four or five lines and type a brief biographical note about yourself. If there's not enough room on the page, type this bionote on a separate sheet and attach it after the last page. This paragraph usually mentions your previous publications—especially if you've written a book—or some personal experience that relates to the subject of the article. For example:

> Thomas Clark is editor of *Writer's Digest* magazine and the author of *Queries and Submissions* (Writer's Digest Books).

Check the magazine you're writing for to determine the appropriate length and tone. Some editors have a penchant for the wry comment, as in:

> Thomas Clark is editor of *Writer's Digest*, where he keeps a collection of really bad query letters he's folded into paper airplanes.

(Important note: I don't really.)

Including sidebars

A sidebar is a short article that accompanies a feature article. The sidebar's topic is related to the main feature's, but it expands on some interesting minor issue or piece of the topic. The sidebar's material could possibly have been included in the main article, but the fit would not have been a smooth one. A personal narrative on one woman's fight against breast cancer might include a sidebar listing sources for more information and a second on how to perform a routine self-exam. The armchair travelogue on the Great Smoky Mountains might include a box of "When You Go" information about park hours and recommended hotels or a roundup of the kazillion outlet stores in nearby Pigeon Forge, Tennessee. All four of these sidebars present information that readers will want, yet all would have disrupted their main articles' flow.

Check your sample issues to determine if your market routinely breaks off text into sidebars. They generally appear in a shaded box adjacent to the feature; part of the sidebars' appeal is as a graphic element to catch the browsing reader's attention.

If your market uses sidebars, look for relevant material within your topic that could make a fascinating side trip for the magazine's readers. Maybe it will be a list (of resources, of bests and worsts, of hot tips— any sort of numbered grouping) or a quiz or a chart or a couple paragraphs of fact-laden text. If you find something appropriate, write it up and include the piece with your manuscript. Don't worry if you didn't promise the sidebar in your original query letter or if the editor didn't ask for one in the assignment. An unexpected sidebar is the sort of "extra service" touch that editor's remember fondly when making future assignments. (It may even earn you a few additional dollars.)

The manuscript format for a sidebar resembles the front page of an article, except I simply type a slugline in the top left-hand corner of the page, continuing the page numbering from the last page of the manuscript. I've seen writers go the whole front-page route and type another address block, and that's acceptable. But I think the running page number in the slugline binds the total package together.

Drop down the page and center the sidebar's title as you did on page one. Instead of a byline, type "Sidebar to" and the title of your article, as in:

"Sidebar Formats"
Sidebar to "Queries and Submissions"

You shouldn't need more than two or three pages for your sidebar, as these pieces generally run no longer than 10 percent of the main article's length. Continue the slugline on succeeding pages. Many magazines use the writer's initials at the end of a sidebar as a sort of byline. Check your target magazine's style and follow that. If initials or a byline aren't used, type "The End" again.

If you submit more than one sidebar, start the next one on a new page (but continuing the page numbering sequence). Three sidebars would be the most I'd ever submit, and then only with a major feature article. (You want the editor to believe you have *some* self-control.) One is plenty; add a second and third only if each covers completely different aspects of the topic.

The last review

Computers have eased writers' typing burdens considerably. Revisions no longer require the complete retyping of a manuscript; you change a word and enter a command, and a flawless manuscript drops into the tray.

Is it really flawless? Just because you've mastered your software's spell-checker, don't assume your word processor has acquired the gift of discerning whether you meant *war* or *wary*, *not* or *note*, *choose* or *chose*, or any other word that is absolutely correct in its spelling yet absolutely wrong in its typing.

No matter how tempting it is to punch in the Print command and forget it, *read* your article on paper before you mail it. Printers get rambunctious and occasionally drop off a line or two. And I simply see mistakes better on the page than on the monitor—I guess it's the crystal contrast of black letters on white paper. An occasional crossed-out word and penciled-in correction will hurt your credibility much less than a flock of misspellings.

The complete package

The hour is at hand; you've polished your manuscript so thoroughly that the pages sparkled as they landed in the printer tray. Finally, it's ready for the editor's review.

But what goes into the envelope?

We'll start with the manuscript: Are you sending your only copy? *Don't.* Make a high-quality photocopy of your work before you send it. (In fact, consider sending the photocopy instead of your original. Patches of correction fluid don't show up on copied pages, and today's plain paper copiers allow you to load the machine with whatever quality paper you prefer. And you'll have the original for future copies.) The awful truth is that manuscripts are lost in the mail, do fall into the trash can, will get ketchup and coffee spilled on them, and do grow ragged as they're passed from mailbox to mailbox, desk to desk, hand to hand. The wonderful truth is we're only talking paper here. Keep a copy, and dare editors, clerks and postal machines to do their worst.

Even if you work on computer and have the text on your hard disk (*and* a floppy), keep a paper copy of your manuscript handy. Computers crash, floppies fail, printers die—and always when you need a new copy. Besides, if your editor calls to discuss the manuscript, it's nice to pull page seven out of a file instead of having to boot up your computer and find the right disk and run through the file before you can hear her comments.

If your editor works with disk submissions, ask for her preferences in preparing the file. The general rule is to prepare a file as free of special coding as possible, but it seems every magazine's computer system has different requirements. Once you've prepared the file, copy it onto a new, blank disk for submission. Today's three and a half-inch disks absorb a fair amount of punishment, but even they benefit from some protection; tape them to a piece of cardboard or pack them in a special disk mailer. And, of course, you must still send a properly formatted manuscript. (But you knew that.)

Paper clip together the pages of your manuscript.

Magazine requirements vary on this point, but many editors expect to see a source list or other information that will help the magazine fact-check your article. A good source list includes the name, title, address and phone number of each person quoted in the article, as well as complete information on any other source that provided information used in the article. One approach guaranteed to win a fact-checker's heart is an annotated copy of the manuscript, with each fact footnoted. This is particularly useful when you're writing about potentially controversial subjects. For most manuscripts, though, a complete source list is enough.

If you have graphics for the article, now is the time to send them—within reason. If this is an unsolicited manuscript, don't send artwork that is irreplaceable. (Honestly, slush doesn't always get the respectful treatment it deserves.) If you must have artwork returned, don't send it until the editor invites it. Package what you do send carefully; 8″ × 10″ photos are less likely to slip away from your manuscript than snapshot-size prints, and slides are protected from damage in plastic sleeves. Keep copies in your files of all charts, sketches, maps, graphs and other illustrations you send to the editor.

And don't forget a self-addressed envelope of sufficient size—with sufficient postage affixed—to bring the whole package home. There is a school of thought that says if your submission is invited, you need not enclose an SASE. To which I respond, "Why pinch pennies?" If my work is rejected, I don't want some editorial assistant trying to decide what's important enough to send back or waiting for a box of big-enough envelopes to arrive from Supply. Plus, it's a matter of dotting all the *i*'s and crossing all the *t*'s. When you submit work to an editor, you send an SASE. It's Rule #2, right after "Know your market."

Seal your manuscript, et al., in an envelope roomy enough to hold it all. One of my quirks concerns thick manuscripts stuffed into business-size envelopes. Show your manuscript a little respect! If you're sending more than five or six pages, lay the pages flat in a 9″ × 12″ envelope. I know one freelancer who backs every submission with a piece of cardboard. That's extreme (and expensive—that cardboard means an additional stamp). But it makes a statement about the high regard in which this writer holds his work.

One statement you don't need to make is with an excessive amount of tape applied to the flap of your envelope. You aren't sealing up Fort Knox; in fact, your envelope is meant to be opened eventually. Heel your paranoia, and trust the manufacturer's glue to do its job.

Address the package to the editor who offered the assignment, and mark the envelope "Requested Material." This should prevent your work from landing in the slush pile, even if the editor fails to recognize your name and return address when skimming the day's mail. If your submission is unsolicited, it may well end up in the slush pile. But you'll lessen the chance of that fate by addressing it to a specific editor. (For tips on finding the right editor, see chapter three.)

If your deadline is a week or more away, you can safely depend on first-class mail to deliver your manuscript. If the sands of time are hitting you with a bit more force, don't hesitate to call on an overnight delivery service. But if it doesn't absolutely, positively have to be there overnight, check out such services as United Parcel Service's Two-Day Delivery or the U.S. Postal Service's Priority Mail. Both will gain you speed without costing you the entire article fee.

And for those articles that absolutely, positively had to be there today—and weren't—technology gave us the fax. Many neighborhood print shops offer access to a fax machine at something approaching reasonable rates. But call the editor before you hit "Send." She may have some flexibility in the schedule. But don't make a habit of cutting deadlines so close.

In the course of your writing career, you may hit upon a hundred more questions regarding how a particular manuscript should be formatted or shipped. If the article is assigned and the issue at hand seems major, call your editor or her assistant for counsel. If the article is unsolicited or you recognize the point is minor, follow your instincts. After all, you, too, are a professional. Consider your options and decide how you'd prefer to see the manuscript.

CONCLUSION

O nce your manuscript package is entrusted to the letter carrier and the tides of fortune, it's time to sit back and congratulate yourself. Any number of events may lay ahead—including revision phone calls and late-night rewriting—and fame and fortune may still choose to keep their distance. But you've accomplished a task: You've progressed from a stack of sample issues and a page of writer's guidelines to a completed manuscript that some editor is expecting. Your query letter sold the idea, and your manuscript will bring home the check. (Hopefully on acceptance.)

If this was your first run around the track, savor this feeling. You haven't reached the finish line, of course; the time to break out the bubbly is still to come—although it may come as soon as the editor's response. Try not to dwell on that moment, however; you just may give in to the strong temptation to mug the letter carrier each day. Accept that the editor's decision is out of your hands. But if you continued to employ in the writing of the article the knowledge you used in the writing of the query letter, the editor who loved your query will probably love your article, too. And if not this time, then soon.

If this was not your first lap, then you know what you face. A little pat on the back, a bit of self-indulgent plotting about how to blow the check. Then it's back to the writer's guidelines that arrived in yesterday's mail and a new stack of sample issues. You have this idea, and this just might be the right audience to do something with it. . . .

Successful freelancing isn't a one-shot proposition. You write, you sell, and you write again. But each article will be a different experience. That first article may be on safety in the home, and the next one is on Hawaiian rain forests, and the third is on mega-aquariums. The world truly *is* your oyster; you can pluck the pearl of an idea from any spot on it.

The freedom to explore the seven seas is one of freelancing's great joys—and one of its most dangerous temptations. In the rush to stake out new territory, a lot of us forget to tend the fertile beds we've already harvested, and which can be returned to again and again. As an editor, each time I make an assignment to an unfamiliar writer, I wonder if this one will be a "good writer"—one who cultivates my magazine as a home for his writing even as I cultivate him as a provider of new ideas and insights. Will I see his second idea? His third? And beyond? Will he find a place in the stable, perhaps back there on the left where the genre writer who hit the big time once wrote?

It's one of the sales profession's hoariest clichés: The easiest business is repeat business. An editor who liked your writing once will probably like it again; the magazine that you once fit into will probably find you a comfortable fit once again. There's more to it, of course, than just knocking on the door and announcing, "I'm back!" You must again brainstorm and tinker and hone and shape, but you'll do so with the assurance that once before you got it right. You knew this market.

Do this successfully a couple more times, and you just might find yourself with an assignment that *didn't* require you to brainstorm and tinker and hone and shape. It required you only to open the editor's letter or take her phone call. The assignment is yours, and the pay will be yours, but the idea was hers. And she brought it to *your* door and asked you to write it: "You did such a good job with the last piece that I knew you'd bring just the right touch to this one."

What a lovely thing to say about your favorite writer.

Back in chapter six, when I examined the résumé section of the query letter, I mentioned that freelancing was unusual for requiring the best work from its novices. It's always struck me as slightly unfair that a writer's very first letters must be good enough to break through an editor's familiarity with her known writers and the predictability that comes from working with known quantities—even though the new writer is still learning how to make words do his bidding. Happily, it doesn't take long to become one of the familiar, one of the known. And with that status comes a reduced reliance on query writing; even the sketchiest outline of an idea might earn you an assignment.

When I began this book, I wrote several writers I work with to ask them for copies of their successful query letters. And quite a few called back to say, "Ya know, Tom, most of those are packed away somewhere. I just don't write that many queries anymore because mostly, well, editors keep me busy with their ideas. Sorry about that. . . ."

Right now you may find it hard to imagine a time when you won't have to sweat through multiple drafts of a query letter that you'll still ask a priest to pray over. But it can happen. With determination, you can make it happen for you.

It starts with the writer's guidelines and the sample issues and the brainstorming and tinkering and honing and shaping. And it starts with writing about what you know. And the multiple drafts. And the "Nos" that come more frequently than the "Yeses." And the on-spec assignments that turn into acceptance letters. You can make it happen by knowing each market you approach as well as its editor and turning that knowledge into article idea after article idea.

Good things come to those who work for them. I wish you good things.

INDEX